CELEBRATING CHOPIN AND PADEREWSKI

BY
MAREK ŻEBROWSKI

Figure 1: A map of the Commonwealth of Poland-Lithuania, showing the largest territorial extent of this once largest country in Europe that stretched from the Baltic to the Black Sea. Polish Music Center Archives, USC

To my piano teachers with boundless gratitude

for sharing the great tradition of piano playing

CONCEPT & EDITORIAL SUPERVISION

Ministry of Foreign Affairs of the Republic of Poland
Department of Public and Cultural Diplomacy

RECORDING LICENSE

DUX Recording Producers
Morskie Oko 2 | 02-511 Warsaw | Poland
http://www.dux.pl | dux@dux.pl

RECORDING SUPERVISION & SOUND ENGINEERING

Małgorzata Polańska & Lech Tołwiński

MASTERING

Dorota Tarnowska-Antosik

COVER DESIGN

Agnieszka Zakrzewska

LAYOUT

Rafał Dymerski

PRINTING & BINDING

Zakład Poligraficzny Serigraph Sp. z o.o.

ISBN 978-83-919769-4-4

Table of Contents

~ INTRODUCTION ~

The occasion for this particular essay on the founding fathers of Polish pianism presented itself with something as inevitable as a stroke of the midnight bell, when the year 2009 receded into history. 2010, besides being an interesting and round number, happens to be the year of two important and just as round birthday anniversaries in the history of Polish music: Frederic Chopin's bicentennial and Ignacy Jan Paderewski's sesquicentennial. Whilst a number of anniversary tributes for each of these great musicians will joyfully be made this year, to the best of my knowledge the comparisons of Chopin and Paderewski—as pianists, composers, and individuals—has received much less attention. The idea of writing such a study was suggested to me by my friends in the Ministry of Foreign Affairs in Poland during the waning months of last year. Preliminary discussions about writing an homage to two of Poland's greatest musicians were held in Warsaw and, after weighing all kinds of possible approaches to the subject, plans for this modest tribute were finalized last December after my meetings at the Ministry with Mariusz Brymora and his associate, Adam Zarzycki. The idea of adding Paderewski's historical recordings of Chopin to my book was then proposed and, in turn, provided a key for how to approach the task at hand. Chopin as performed by Paderewski was the strongest link and the best reason to attempt this summary and, in the short time allotted for its completion (after all anniversaries come and go very quickly), led to what the readers will find on the following pages.

Much of the information contained herein can be found elsewhere, and yet setting the lives of Chopin and Paderewski side by side led to the emergence of many fascinating parallels and similarities heretofore unexplored. Certain larger themes that strongly defined these two artists— Poland's glorious history and musical tradition, the cultural and political scene in Poland under partitions, and the always controversial question of artist's role in political life—proved worthy of at least a passing comment of these pages. Certainly much more can be written on these topics, for each of them opens a landscape rich in detail and provides a wider perspective on events and facts that are generally known, but beg further exploration. This fascination of discovering anew the road well travelled is what drove the author's task. I hope that—in the same measure—it will sustain the reader's interest as well.

Marek Żebrowski
Los Angeles, 1 March 2010

CELEBRATING CHOPIN AND PADEREWSKI

Chapter One

Chopin, Paderewski, and the Rise of the Piano Virtuoso

Whenever the phrase "Polish Piano School" is heard or a discussion of Polish pianism takes place, two names instantly come to mind—that of Frederic Chopin (1810-1849) and Ignacy Jan Paderewski (1860-1941). In various ways and each during his own time, these two great pianists and composers defined a venerable tradition of performance and interpretation that is now universally recognized and cherished. Reflecting in greater detail upon the lives and careers of Chopin and Paderewski leads one to realize how they became the milestones of musical achievement for generations of musicians throughout the world. Naturally, any analysis of Chopin's and Paderewski's impact on the history of music must place them in the context of the artistic and political landscape they inhabited in their country of birth and in their adopted homelands.

The influence of Chopin and Paderewski on the musicians who followed in their footsteps was immense and it continues to cast its magic spell upon the young pianists today. There are many excellent reasons for such an unqualified verdict of history. Chopin was really the first great composer and pianist who in his all too rare public performances stunned the audiences with his exquisite touch and new sonorities, as well as beautiful and refined melodies and harmonies. Chopin's poetic virtuosity and absolute command of piano technique were envied by Romantic-era virtuosos and composers such as Felix Mendelssohn (1809-1847) or Franz Liszt (1811-1886). In addition to his inspired piano playing, Chopin's consummate compositions elicited the very highest praise from such fellow composers and noted music critics as Robert Schumann (1810-1856) and Hector Berlioz (1803-1869).

Following Chopin half a century later, Paderewski began his life in music as a salon virtuoso who at first entertained the intellectual elites of Victorian-era Poland. Gradually building on his growing reputation and relentlessly pursuing an international career, after graduating from the Music Institute in Warsaw Paderewski studied composition in Berlin and later moved to study piano in Vienna with the famed pianist, composer and pedagogue, Teodor Leschetizky (1830-1915). After his stunning 1888 Paris debut Paderewski began to tour Europe with concerts. Following the example of Liszt, a veteran of countless European concert stages, and Anton Rubinstein (1829-1894), one of the first eminent European pianists to tour North America, Paderewski became the first great pianist in history to travel the world so extensively. With his concerts throughout Europe, North and South America, South Africa, Australia and New Zealand, Paderewski set the performance standards with his careful selection of repertoire and charted the course for modern day touring and recording artists. Paderewski's recital programs always featured a generous offering of Chopin's music, ranging from the more intimate Nocturnes, Mazurkas, and Etudes to the more substantial Polonaises, Ballades, and Sonatas. In his choice of repertoire, which Paderewski performed worldwide, he established the fact that performing a group of Chopin's compositions in recital reflected a measure of pianistic accomplishment. As a result, for every aspiring young pianist, mastering of a large portion of Chopin's opus and presenting it in recital became a *sine qua non* requirement for the validation of a performing career.

Chopin's music had occupied a large part of the concert repertoire ever since it was published during the first half of the nineteenth century and it never went out of style. Programs by such early touring virtuosos as Louis Moreau Gottschalk (1829-1869) or Anton Rubinstein, who devoted large portions of their programs to Chopin's oeuvre, prove that the public demanded and expected to hear Chopin alongside the other classics like Bach, Mozart or Beethoven. Particularly noteworthy is the example of Rubinstein who finished his American tour with a series of seven gargantuan recital programs given over a nine-day period in New York City in May of 1873. Each of these featured the most important works from the pantheon of composers: there were recitals of Bach, Mozart, Beethoven, and an entire recital devoted to Chopin's music. To this day, an all-Chopin program is an accepted standard for programming, on par with an all-Bach or all-Beethoven offering. Recitals dedicated exclusively to works of practically all other composers appear on many recordings but are heard much more rarely in concert.

The pilgrimage of students and disciples seeking the source of arguably the most beautiful romantic piano music had already commenced during Chopin's lifetime. The eleven-year old Anton Rubinstein came from Russia to Paris with hopes of meeting the most important composers living there, as the French capital was unquestionably the center of the music world at the time. Rubinstein also wanted to study at the Paris Conservatoire. Although the objections of its director, Luigi Cherubini (1760-1842), proved an obstacle to the young Russian prodigy's enrollment at the Conservatoire, this setback did not prevent Rubinstein's debut recital at Salle Érard in Paris in 1840 in presence of Chopin and Liszt. Chopin later invited the young boy to his salon and played for him. As a result, throughout his career Rubinstein

frequently featured Chopin's compositions in his recitals.

A rather similar fate awaited the thirteen-year old Louis Moreau Gottschalk only two years later. Gottschalk was the first American virtuoso to arrive in Paris with plans of studying at the Conservatoire. He too was dismissed

Figure 2: The entrance to the Paris Conservatoire building on Rue du Faubourg-Poissonière in 1848. Originally founded in 1784 as the *École royale de chant et de declamation*, the institution had changed its charter and mission in 1795 and was officially renamed *Conservatoire national de musique et de déclamation*. A library was added in 1808 and a concert hall with a seating for a 1000 and excellent acoustics was dedicated in 1811. In the mid-1850s the Conservatoire was moved to another building on the corner of Rue du Conservatoire. Private collection. All rights reserved

by Cherubini, but met and played for Chopin and became his friend. Gottschalk was also known for programming Chopin's music in his recitals, not only in Europe but also in the United States, where he was recognized as the New World's most important pianist after his return to America in 1853. Writing in his diaries a decade later, Gottschalk reflected on how popular Chopin's music had become in the United States:

> Since Liszt has given the word of command to the Germans, Chopin has all at once become classical. His forms, which before they regarded—without understanding them—as whimsical, his harmonies so worked up, have become so many perfect models. I do not complain for my part, having been one of the old Chopinists, but what I deplore is the frightful abuse that is made of Chopin's formulas. There is not a small pianist-composer who does not think himself called upon to make Chopin mazurkas, Chopin nocturnes, Chopin polonaises—it has become an epidemic in the United States. They have become masters of Chopin's processes and employ them without discernment in the most trivial melodies. This recalls to me Madame F., who composed music à la Haydn.[1]

Other aspiring artists soon followed by becoming "Chopinists" in Gottschalk's own *bon mot*, and the trail of some of the most prominent names among the pantheon of pianists—Vladimir de Pachmann, Raoul Pugno, Ignacy Jan Paderewski, Maurycy Rosenthal, Sergei Rachmaninov, Alfred Cortot, Ignacy Friedman, Raoul Koczalski, Artur Rubinstein, Mieczysław Horszowski, Claudio Arrau, Vladimir Horowitz, Dinu Lipatti, Vladimir Ashkenazy, Martha Argerich, Maurizio Pollini, Murray Perahia, Krystian Zimerman, Evgeny Kissin, and Rafał Blechacz—leads us from Chopin directly to the present day. Beginning with de Pachmann (1848-1933)—one of the earliest direct links to Chopin's performance tradition—all of these artists have produced a number of recordings that enable us to trace the stylistic development of interpreting Chopin's music.

This magnificent tradition was also possible because of one crucial technological invention that took place in the early decades of the eighteenth century—the emergence of the modern piano from its direct predecessors, the Baroque era harpsichord and clavichord. The new instrument's name, *pianoforte*, was an abbreviation of the descriptive Italian term *clavicembalo col piano e forte* [a soft and loud harpsichord]. Equipped with hammers that hit the strings rather than the string-plucking tangents or quills on older keyboard instruments like the harpsichord or a clavichord, the sound of the *pianoforte* could be varied depending on the kind of touch used by the performer on the keys. Instantly, a wide range of sounds levels and new expressive horizons had opened up to performers.

Bartolomeo Cristofori (1655-1731), a harpsichord maker employed by Prince Ferdinand de Medici, designed just such a mechanism that transferred the performer's touch from the key to the strings by means of rapidly rising and retreating hammers. Dating from the 1720s, his earliest instruments already have the early version of the modern piano action. As soon as Cristofori's mechanism became known among the builders of keyboard instruments, a series of rapid improvements followed. With such makers as Silbermann (whose instruments were introduced to Bach), Stein, Streicher, and Walter, southern Germany and Austria became the leading regions for piano development in Europe. The demise of the harpsichord was swift—whereas Johann Sebastian Bach (1685-1750) was primarily known as an organist and a harpsichord virtuoso, Wolfgang Amadeus Mozart (1756-1791) was a *fortepiano* performer, who composed all of his Sonatas and Concertos for the latest models of keyboard instruments produced in Vienna.

Demands by composers-performers for more powerful and longer-lasting sound led to continuous advances in piano design. The Industrial Revolution introduced new methods for producing high quality steel piano strings and cast-iron frames. Soon, larger and more robust-sounding instruments were developed by the English piano maker, Broadwood, whose pianos were used by Joseph Haydn (1732-1809) during his visits in London in the 1790s, and Ludwig van Beethoven (1770-1827), who—among his fourteen pianos—owned a Broadwood grand, given to him by the manufacturer.[2]

The ever-more complex keyboard compositions of Mozart, Haydn and especially Beethoven led to a constant quest in perfecting the sound, range, and inner mechanism—the so-called "action"—of the piano. In addition to Austrian, German and English piano makers, two prominent manufacturers emerged in France and, by the end of the 1820s, Pleyel pianos from Paris began to compete with instruments made in London and Vienna. Whilst Pleyel pianos with their silvery tone and relatively light touch were Chopin's favorite instruments, Liszt preferred to use the bigger-sounding and somewhat stiffer Érard, another venerable French manufacturer, who introduced in 1821 the so-called "double escape mechanism" that allowed for the quick succession of repeated notes, an innovation that became standard equipment for all pianos since then.[3] Further improvements included fitting the pianos with foot-operated pedals that could lift dampers from the strings (giving the sound more volume) or shift them to only one or two strings (to produce very soft sounds). Modern scientific theories about sound propagation were applied to the arrangements of strings inside the piano and to the design of the resonance board. Steinway, a company that originated in Germany but made its mark in the United States in the 1860s, became yet another honored name in the history of piano and undoubtedly has made the finest instruments in the world since the 1870s.

These refinements—which continued throughout the nineteenth century—gave an unprecedented opportunity to the piano performer to evoke a wide range of tone-colors and great variety of sounds from the instrument. The expansion of the piano's range of registers (from the five octave span during Mozart's time to the modern standard of over seven octaves) further enabled various composers-virtuosos to dazzle their audiences with sounds and textures heretofore unobtainable from the harpsichord or earlier versions of the piano from the eighteenth century.

As an expressive instrument, the piano quite naturally became a favorite instrument of the Romantic era. It could be played softly and tenderly but, when necessary, it was also capable of filling large public spaces with a powerful sound on its own. The resonant tone available throughout the piano's spectrum of dynamics was far superior to the harpsichord's delicate timbre. As a result, the harpsichord—an instrument perfectly suited to the intimate musical gatherings of the eighteenth century—could never become the solo instrument for large public concerts to the extent that a pianoforte could. Mozart was first to grasp this fact and to explore the expressive possibilities of the redesigned instrument by writing over two dozen Concertos for piano and orchestra. His incredibly imaginative approach to the relationship between a piano and the ensemble that accompanied it represents a lasting achievement in the genre. Mozart's Piano Concertos paved the way for Beethoven's Concertos and, in turn, inspired a plethora of compositions by other pianists-composers of the Romantic era, who continued to transform the role of the piano on a concert stage.

With its capacity of producing an almost infinite variety of sounds, moods and emotions, the nineteenth century piano enabled the Romantic artist to communicate more intimately with his audience. The Romantic era was a time of revolution in art, music, literature, and politics. Passion and freedom—as opposed to reason and restraint—ruled the day, and passionately expressed emotions ruled the arts. Imagination and novelty were judged more important than logic and experience. A synthesis of various art forms often served as an inspiration and a goal for the Romantic artist, be it in music, literature, or painting. Narrative devices borrowed from literature reshaped musical forms, and the allure of storytelling in such genres as the tone poem or the ballade stimulated the imagination of composers and listeners.

Just like the Romantic literature and art, Romantic music often concerned itself with supernatural phenomena, sought to describe exotic places, and attempted to illustrate fantastic events. Unprecedented virtuosity and many special effects—rapid passagework throughout the whole compass of the keyboard, orchestral sonorities, myriad shades of color achieved by the discriminating touch and highly-refined use of pedals—became a trademark of the Romantic piano virtuoso. Old instruments like the violin could also be played in entirely new ways, as demonstrated by the legendary performer Niccolò Paganini (1782-1840), who transformed the Baroque-era violin into a vehicle capable of extreme virtuosity as well as profound expression. Paganini's spectacular recitals in Vienna and Warsaw (where he met Chopin) in the late 1820s and in Paris in the early 1830s galvanized the imagination of piano virtuosos and other prominent musicians of the day, and almost instantly were reflected in a variety of brilliant piano effects. Chopin's concerts in Vienna in 1829 and 1831 and his arrival in Paris later that year followed Paganini's legendary series of ten recitals in the French capital during March and April of 1831.

Paganini's career developed on the cusp of the Romantic era and provided other instrumental virtuosos with a ready-made formula to follow. It was a propitious time for a musical career, since during the first half of the nineteenth century public concerts were on the rise and music conservatories had opened in various European capitals. Concerts of all kinds—a domain of private entertainment previously reserved for the aristocratic and clerical circles—had now entered the public sphere and were organized and appreciated by an ever-widening portion of society. The figure of the instrumental virtuoso dazzling the crowds with assorted musical and technical accomplishments packed into his latest compositions and receiving fabulous honoraria was a phenomenon that emerged during the Romantic era. Artists like Chopin, Liszt, Rubinstein or Paderewski who followed Paganini to the public forum, were among the first international celebrities to be treated like figures in the top echelons of the entertainment world today.

The public viewed Romantic virtuosos as heroic figures who led extraordinary lives and whose adventures became the harbingers of social change. Chopin's decade-long relationship with George Sand—a writer of considerable fame and a divorced mother of two who engaged in several affairs with public figures—was hardly an exception. Liszt's private life was even more colorful, with highlights that included a liaison with a married countess, children born out of wedlock, and Liszt's entry into a religious order for the last two decades of his life. Liszt was not alone in his unprecedented lifestyle, since public pursuits of their loved ones (as in the case of Berlioz and Schumann) were quickly becoming a trend among the Romantic-era musicians, adding to their exalted position as barrier-breakers in art and trailblazers in the realm of the domestic life.

Romantic artists began taking the stage at exactly the moment of profound political transformations in Europe. The French Revolution of 1789 followed by the Napoleonic era and the return towards absolute monarchy after Napoleon's demise provided a powerful context for the Romantic artists' imagination. Beethoven's admiration for Napoleon and his subsequent fury after Napoleon's betrayal of the Republican ideals is well-known. Richard Wagner's direct involvement in the 1848 Revolution in Germany led to his escape to Switzerland as he was about to be arrested by Dresden police. Chopin left Poland just before the November 1830 Uprising but was nonetheless profoundly affected by its tragic outcome, as witnessed by letters to his family and his exceptionally fiery compositions, including the famous Etude Op. 10 no. 12 and the B-minor Scherzo that date from the years 1830-1832.

Poland's political situation throughout the nineteenth century was particularly difficult, as this once largest country in Europe was erased from the map by its neighbors by the late 1790s. To this day the so-called partitions of Poland represent the most egregious land grab in world history. This unprecedented action by Russia, Prussia and Austria—the trio of absolute monarchies surrounding Poland—stemmed from their deep concern about the democratic developments that included the promulgation of Poland's very progressive Constitution in May of 1791. It was only the second written constitution in the world (after the American Constitution) and Poland's conservative neighbors simply could not envision a democratic state on their borders. From the late 1790s until the end of World War I, Poland existed only in the hearts of its native sons and daughters, as its territories were administered by Russia (in the East), Prussia (in the West and North), and Austria (in the South). Almost every Polish artist living during this time accepted the patriotic mission of proclaiming his homeland's identity through his literary, musical or artistic creations. Chopin's free and poetic transformation of such traditional Polish genres as the Mazurka or the Polonaise was not only a quintessential musical response but also a deeply patriotic statement. Without a doubt, Chopin's contemporaries clearly understood his intentions. Referring to the Tsar Nicolas I who brutally crushed the November 1830 Uprising

in Poland, Robert Schumann famously wrote that "… If the mighty autocratic monarch of the North knew what a dangerous enemy threatened him in Chopin's works, in the simple melodies of his Mazurkas, he would forbid this music. Chopin's works are cannon buried under flowers!"[4]

Already during Chopin's lifetime his music had made a strong and effective political statement. Schumann's remarks on the subject expressed in one of the articles he wrote for the *Neue Zeitschrift für Musik* are very much to the point:

All Polish compositions which have recently appeared have been more or less influenced by Chopin. Through him Poland has obtained a seat and vote in the great musical parliament of nations. Annihilated politically, it will ever continue to flower in our art.[5]

Such a reaction underscores the role of the Romantic musician as not merely an artist but also as a potential agent of political change. Just like Chopin, from his youth Paderewski had envisioned a larger role for himself and his music:

…I had a real ambition to become an artist… I was *sure* that I would attain something, and it must be said now that my true object—my great object—already, at the age of seven, was to be useful to my own country, which was then, as you know, partitioned, having no existence of her own and very oppressed. My great hope was to become *somebody*, and so to help Poland. That was over and above all my artistic aspirations. I was always ready and planning to fight for Poland, and my sister and I were always playing soldier when we were not playing duets! Even from my sixth year my head was filled with dreams and hopes for Poland. I longed to go forth and liberate my country. As children, Antonina and I played "soldier" nearly every day. My part was, I must say, the most interesting one, for I, of course, was the warrior and rode the horse—the charger on which I set forth to victory. The steed was represented by a long stick on which my sister arranged a bag stuffed with all kinds of things to represent the horse's head, even the ears. My costume too, the Polish uniform, was made by my sister of white and red paper with a red square cap. The crowning glory, the sword, was a piece of wood cut with my jack-knife. On this splendid charger I rode all over the house pretending to fight a battle. And my patriotism was always encouraged by my father and my teachers. There were no protests to our playing soldier in the house. Patriotism and music marched hand in hand. My life began like that.[6]

Remarkably indeed, Paderewski realized his childhood dreams since his destiny was to become not only one of the most prominent pianists of all times, but also a statesman and politician par excellence. The fall of monarchies and autocratic regimes that began with the French Revolution took over a century to complete, but by the end of World War I, the Tsar, the Kaiser, and the Emperor were defeated and democratically elected governments sprang all over Europe. Like no other leader in the history of his country, Paderewski was instrumental in ending Poland's partitions, even though the question of eastern borders (that included his homeland province of Podolia) and the issue of the Danzig corridor were never satisfactorily settled during the Peace Conference in Versailles.[7] Nonetheless, Poland became a free and democratic state for the period of twenty years before World War II laid waste to Poland and to Paderewski's political accomplishments.

Another important factor in popularity of the Romantic piano music was the rapid rise in public education and the unprecedented interest in learning the piano among the newly-emergent middle classes. This was the same public that attended concerts, heartily cheered and idolized the virtuosos and hoped that by offering music education to their children, they—and their families—could enjoy the pleasures of music to an even greater extent. Looking at it from the perspective of time, George Bernard Shaw in *The Religion of the Pianoforte* (1894) stated that, "The pianoforte is the most important of all musical instruments: its invention was to music what the invention of printing was to poetry." In his statement Shaw deftly encapsulated the indispensible role of piano in the enlightenment of the society, as learning the instrument and reading music were the essential steps leading to a deeper enjoyment of music and to becoming a true connoisseur. The great performers' accomplishments were all the more inspiring to the lesser mortals who spent considerable time and capital on learning to play the instrument themselves. Conservatories began to open all across Europe, including Paris (1795), Prague (1811), Vienna (1817), and Leipzig (1843). Virtuoso pianist and composer, Felix Mendelssohn was the first director of the Leipzig Conservatory and he laid out a three year curriculum that became standard throughout Germany.[8] For the ever-widening circles of society, the piano became something akin to the modern entertainment center: the latest symphonies by Haydn, Mozart, and Beethoven were transcribed for the piano and often cast in a 4-hand arrangement for two players that enabled talented amateurs to entertain their families and friends with the latest orchestral repertoire at private musical soirees. Faced with a strong demand for pianos, the number of piano manufacturers rose rapidly throughout Europe. Within a few decades many ordinary homes—not only the palaces and residents of the elite—had pianos installed in the drawing rooms.

Many nineteen century artists cultivated the informal atmosphere of salons, where aristocratic circles happily mingled with a more Bohemian crowd. Franz Schubert (1797-1828) was one of the composers whose music was almost exclusively introduced to a select group of friends in various Viennese salons. Chopin also preferred the intimate salon setting and, after moving to Paris, appeared in public only on rare occasions. Likewise, Paderewski's early career included many private performances in Warsaw's salons and in the fashionable mountain resort Zakopane, where he became the toast of the Polish intellectual and social elites.[9]

1 Louis Moreau Gottschalk: *Notes of a Pianist*, Princeton University Press, 2006, p. 193

2 James Parakilas: *Piano Roles—Three Hundred Years of Life with the Piano*. Yale University Press, 1999, p. 125

3 Gottschalk briefly discussed the differences between Pleyel and Érard pianos in his diaries: "Erard's, whose tone is robust, strong, heroic, slightly metallic, is adapted exclusively to the powerful action of Liszt. Pleyel's, less sonorous but poetical and, so to speak, languishing and feminine, corresponds to the elegiac style and frail organization of Chopin." *Notes of a Pianist*, Princeton University Press, 2006, p. 244

4 See Robert Schumann, *On Music and Musicians*, p. 132

5 Ibid., pp. 145-146

6 Paderewski and Lawton: *Memoirs*, p. 16

7 Paderewski's close friend and a student, Zygmunt Stojowski, expressed in the article about Paderewski written in 1935 for *Życie Muzyczne i Teatralne* [Journal of Music and Theatre] that: "I remember the note of sadness when he told me about his worldwide campaign to regain Polish political rights and independence, but could not lay a claim to the lands of his ancestors, since 'asking for too much meant risking everything.'"

8 James Parakilas: *Piano Roles—Three Hundred Years of Life with the Piano*. Yale University Press, 1999, p. 154

9 See Helena Modjeska's *Memories and Impressions*, p. 464-468

CHAPTER TWO

THE FORMATIVE YEARS

Figure 3: The manor house in Żelazowa Wola. A 2003 Wikipedia photograph by Wojsyl.

For all their considerable differences—including the times in which they lived, their upbringing and schooling as well as their subsequent lives and careers—Chopin and Paderewski shared many similar traits during the first two decades of their development.

Both were born in the countryside to families of relatively modest means but of great cultivation and interest in the arts. Chopin was born just west of Warsaw in the little hamlet of Żelazowa Wola; Paderewski's birthplace was the village of Kuryłówka in the far southeastern reaches of the Polish province of Podolia, now part of the Ukraine. They were born almost exactly fifty years apart, Chopin on 1 March 1810, Paderewski on 6 November 1860, and their connection to the land with its customs and folk music as well as their strong patriotism, shaped their consciousness and artistic imagination from their earliest years onwards.

Chopin's birthplace is a nicely proportioned eighteenth century manor house that belonged to Count Skarbek and his family. A somewhat unusual chain of events led to Chopin being born in that house. Chopin's father, Nicolas, was French but as a young man had immigrated to Poland from his home province of Lorraine in 1787 and quickly became fluent in Polish. His sympathy for Poland was clearly demonstrated when Nicolas Chopin joined the National Guard to defend Warsaw from Russian attack in 1794. After the partitions of Poland, Nicolas abandoned the idea of returning to France and decided to earn his living as teacher of French in Warsaw. After working for several well-to-do Polish families, he eventually became a tutor for the Skarbeks in 1802. There he met Justyna Krzyżanowska, a distant relative of his employer, who also lived on the estate. She was eleven years younger than Nicolas, attractive and well-educated, and they married in 1806. The Chopins had four children—Ludwika (1807-1855), Fryderyk, Isabella (1811-1881), and Emilia (1813-1827). All four children possessed considerable artistic gifts. Ludwika was an excellent pianist and composer (she too wrote some Mazurkas) and so was Isabella, who in her youth clearly recognized her brother's musical talent. The youngest, Emilia, who died of tuberculosis at the age of fourteen, had a substantial literary talent—she wrote poetry and plays that were later staged with her siblings.

———

Paderewski's family belonged to the landed gentry who lived in central Poland. Following a popular trend, various branches of the family left their ancestral seat during the seventeenth century for the sparsely populated regions of Eastern Ukraine, a territory that belonged to the Polish-Lithuanian Commonwealth at that time. Estates owned by Poles who settled there were large-scale agricultural enterprises and also served as outposts of Polish culture and islands of Catholic faith. With the gradual decline of Poland's political fortunes in the second half of the eighteenth century, these lands were annexed by Russia in three partitions—1772, 1793, and 1795—after which Poland as an independent country ceased to exist. The subsequent policy of imposing Russian language and culture as well as the orthodox faith in the Ukraine was mainly directed against the Poles who lived there. The protests against such discrimination were inevitable and, in spite of the overwhelming odds, Poles rose up against the Russians on several occasions: in 1794, in 1812 (when they supported Napoleon's campaign against Russia), and in two insurrections in 1830 and 1863. All of these valiant uprisings were brutally squashed, with many estates seized by the tsarist government and thousands of Poles exiled to Siberia. Paderewski's father, Jan, belonged to such an impoverished family and had to work as a land agent and estate administrator for the Iwanowski family. The Iwanowskis homestead was a handsome country seat, but the administrator lived in a smaller wooden manor in the village of Kuryłówka, near the town of Zhitomir.[1] Jan Paderewski married Poliksena Nowicka, a daughter of a professor of law at Wilno University who was exiled to Siberia. They had two children, Antonina (1858-1941) and Ignacy Jan, born two years after his sister. A few months after Ignacy's birth, his mother died of an infection; much later in his *Memoirs*, Paderewski could only describe his mother as follows:

According to those who knew her she was very musical. Perhaps it was from her that music came to me. She was very distinguished in appearance I have always heard, and very gentle.[2]

Only two years later, the 1863 Uprising proved to be another traumatic event for young Paderewski. Accused of collaborating with the Polish resistance, Paderewski's father was arrested by a detachment of Cossacks and imprisoned in Kiev. Although he was released a year later, he lost his job with the Iwanowskis and in 1867 moved to a town of Sudyłków, where he continued to raise his family and work on another estate owned by a wealthy Polish family. Soon thereafter, Jan Paderewski married a widow, Anna Tankowska, with whom he later had two children, Józef and Maria.[3]

Figure 4: Railroad station in Zhitomir, Ukraine, the nearest big town to Paderewski's birthplace in a photo taken around 1900. The building was demolished long ago. Source: http://www.volhynia.com/

Music played an important role in Chopin's and Paderewski's households and in their youth both were primarily educated at home.

Figure 5: Warsaw Lyceum. A lithograph reproduced in H. Opieński: *Chopin*. Polish Music Center Archives.

Chopin's father was an amateur flutist and violinist, and throughout his life enjoyed playing chamber music with various friends in Warsaw. Chopin's mother played the piano and taught music on occasion. The Chopin family moved to Warsaw a year after Frederic was born, since Nicolas began to teach French at the newly-opened Warsaw Lyceum and at the School of Artillery and Military Engineering. The Lyceum was located on the grounds of the Saxon Palace in the center of Warsaw, and the Chopin family had an apartment in one of the Palace's wings.

Wojciech Żywny (1756-1842) was Chopin's first piano teacher during the years 1816-1822. Born in Bohemia, Żywny spent most of his life in Poland. Primarily a violinist, he composed a number of chamber works in the classical style, some of which show traces of folk music. Żywny quickly discovered Chopin's overwhelming talent and introduced him to the music of Bach and Mozart, whose works Chopin cherished and performed throughout his life. Already in 1817 Chopin was a local celebrity, whom "connoisseurs declare to be Mozart's successor."[4] Only a year later, after playing his own Military March for the Grand Duke Constantine, Chopin gave his first public performance at a charity concert on 24 February 1818 as a soloist in a Piano

Figure 6: Józef Elsner: Oil on canvas by an unknown author, ca. 1805. Collection of the Frederic Chopin Museum at the Frederic Chopin National Institute. Owned by the Frederic Chopin Society, M/227. Used by permission

Concerto by a Bohemian composer, Adalbert Gyrowetz (1763-1850). This event introduced Chopin to the elite of Warsaw's society and led to him being presented to the celebrated Italian singer, Angelica Catalani, who gave concerts in Warsaw in 1819. Chopin's playing so impressed the visiting artist that she presented her young colleague with a pocket watch inscribed to him.

Chopin's parting gift to his first piano teacher was in the form of a Polonaise in A-flat major presented on Żywny's name day, 23 April 1821. Józef Elsner (1769-1854), a Silesian-born Polish composer of operas, symphonies, and numerous religious works, was Chopin's only other music teacher. Tutored at home until he was thirteen, Chopin initially studied with Elsner privately. Since Chopin's father insisted that his son first receive a thorough grounding in regular academic subjects, Chopin attended the Warsaw Lyceum from 1823 until 1826. Afterwards he entered the Warsaw Conservatory, where for the next three years he studied music with Józef Elsner formally. In 1827 the family moved to an apartment in the Krasiński Palace on Krakowskie Przedmieście, an elegant thoroughfare of stately homes and palaces that led to Warsaw's Royal Castle and the Old Town. This was Chopin's last address in Poland.

During his teenage years, Chopin spent summer holidays as guest of aristocratic families in their country homes. He visited the Skarbeks at Żelazowa Wola and the Dziewanowskis in Szafarnia, a little village in north-central Poland. From there Chopin sent several amusing and well-written letters to his family and friends, formatted as mock-dispatches of the fictional *Szafarnia Courier*. Chopin's close contact with folk music also dates from this time and some of the sketches of music he heard found their way to his compositions in the years to come.

———————

Paderewski's musical education was decidedly more chaotic. He apparently started picking out melodies at the piano when he was three years old. Paderewski's father then engaged a local violinist, Mr. Runowski, to give lessons to Ignacy and his sister Antonina. Mr. Runowski was succeeded by Piotr Sowiński, another local and rather undistinguished musician. When Paderewski was eight years old, his father invited a distant

Figure 7: Manor house in Szafarnia: A contemporary photograph by Ewa Sławińska-Dahlig. Photo Collection of the Frederic Chopin National Institute. Used by permission

relative, Michał Babiański, to live with them and tutor his children. Babiański had returned to Poland after spending several decades in exile in Paris. He taught Paderewski French and Polish grammar, mathematics, geography and history.[5] Still without a proper piano teacher and lacking a rigorous approach to learning piano repertoire, Paderewski spent long hours improvising: "I preferred always to improvise rather than practice. I did not know *how* to practice." The instrument at his home was also quite inferior:

> We had a wretched piano. An old piano made in Vienna by Graff. It was an old small piano with a very weak tone and hoarse in sound and scratchy. However, that was the best we could have then.[6]

Paderewski's other homebound pastimes included reading newspapers to the family and occasionally playing chess with his father. When he was twelve, he gave his first public performance, appearing together with Antonina at a local charity concert. That same year a few more recitals—this time solo performances—followed in the nearby towns of Zaslav and Ostrog.[7] Afterwards Paderewski travelled to Kiev, where he attended concerts and met with some influential members of local society. It was soon decided that he should study music in Warsaw and he travelled there with his father to meet the director of Warsaw Musical Institute, Apolinary Kątski. Paderewski was accepted as a student without the usual entry examination and for a few years lived with the Kerntopf family of piano makers in Warsaw. He struck a close friendship

Figure 8: The town of Zaslav in the Volhynia Province. Source: wikimedia.org/wiki/File:Old_zaslav_postcard.png

with Edward Kerntopf and was able to practice on pianos in the factory warehouse. Studying piano at the Institute however proved difficult, since various teachers were either unwilling or doubtful that Paderewski—already a teenager— could ever become a concert pianist. For the time being Paderewski happily pursued music theory, composition and harmony with Mr. Studziński and Mr. Roguski. He also tried studying flute, oboe, clarinet, bassoon, trumpet and the trombone. This last instrument, according to his teacher, was to be the ticket to Paderewski's musical future:

"Now, my dear boy, listen to me. You are always trying to play *piano*. But why? Piano is useless for you—you have no future with the piano; your future is here, playing the trombone! You are really remarkably gifted for it, and you will earn your livelihood with the trombone, not with the piano. [...] Mark my words."[8]

Because of the violent disagreement with the director over the attendance of orchestra rehearsals (where Paderewski played the first trombone), he was expelled from the Music Institute in 1875. He later returned only to be expelled from school again. Restless and eager to perform and earn some money, at the age of sixteen Paderewski embarked on a tour of northern Poland and Russia with two friends—Mr. Cielewicz, a violinist and Mr. Biernacki, a cellist. Various difficulties with securing adequate pianos and venues for performance led to the cellist's return to Warsaw, but the other two pressed on until they ran out of money in Russia. Paderewski's father had to send the funds that allowed the young pianist to return home and, eventually, to Warsaw to complete his studies. Paderewski finally graduated in 1878, receiving his diploma from Director Kątski after performing Grieg's Piano Concerto with the Institute orchestra.

Paderewski's earliest attempts at composition date from that time and include several short piano pieces—*Valse Mignonne* (dedicated to his composition teacher, Roguski), and a few

Impromptus, Gavottes, and Minuets. His first large scale composition is the Sonata for Violin and Piano, a successful and already mature work, completed in 1879.

———————

Whilst Paderewski only gradually and with great determination succeeded, by the age of eighteen, to obtain a diploma in music and gain limited recognition as an aspiring pianist and composer, Chopin at the same age was already a fully mature artist and, as a composer, had a substantial body of music to present in Poland and aboard. His first published work, the *Rondeau in C minor*, Op. 1, dating from 1825, was quickly followed by a flood of new music. By the time Chopin was twenty, his catalogue of compositions contained a number of Polonaises, Waltzes and miscellaneous short piano pieces, most of which were eventually published only after Chopin's death. The bigger and more ambitious compositions from Chopin's teenage years included the Piano Sonata in C minor, Op. 4, *Rondeau à la Mazur*, Op. 5, some of the Op. 10 Etudes, as well as chamber music (*Introduction and Polonaise brillante* for Cello and Piano, Op. 3 and Piano Trio,

Op. 8), as well as works for piano and orchestra (*Don Giovanni Variations*, Op. 2, *Fantaisie on Polish Airs*, Op. 13, *Rondo à la Krakowiak*, Op. 14, and the two Piano Concertos).

By this time Chopin was a well-known and sought-after performer in the salons of Warsaw. He was also beginning to travel out of town. His first bigger journey—to the Silesian resort town Reinertz (today known as Duszniki-Zdrój)—was made for reasons of health. Chopin travelled with his family mainly for the benefit for Chopin's sister, Emilia, who unsuccessfully fought the onset of tuberculosis. Chopin too was subjected to a "water and whey cure," and wittily described its effects on his health as well as the atmosphere of the resort town in letters to his friend Wilhelm Kolberg in Warsaw:

I have been drinking whey and the local waters for two weeks, and they say that I am looking a little better, but I am said to be getting fat, and am as lazy as ever. […] In the morning, at 6 o'clock at the latest, all the patients are at the wells; then there's an atrocious band of wind players: a dozen caricatures of various types collected together; the head one, a thin bassoonist with a snuffy, spectacled nose, frightens all the ladies that are afraid of horses by playing to the freely perambulating Kur-Gäste. […] After breakfast people usually go for a walk. I walk till 12; then one has to eat dinner, because after dinner one has to go back to Brunn. After dinner there's usually a bigger masquerade than in the morning, because everyone is dressed up, all in different clothes from those of the morning. Again there's vile music, and so it goes till evening. As I have to drink only two glasses of Lau-Brunn after dinner I get home to supper fairly early. After supper I go to bed. So when can I write letters?[9]

In a letter to his music professor, Józef Elsner, Chopin was reassuring about his daily health regimen and then complained:

> The fresh air and the whey which I take very conscientiously have set me up so well that I am quite different from what I was in Warsaw. The magnificent views offered by beautiful Silesia enchant and charm me; but one thing is lacking, for which not all the beauties of Reinertz can compensate me: a good instrument.[10]

Lack of good pianos notwithstanding, the sojourn in Reinertz also provided an opportunity for Chopin to play two benefit recitals at the Kurhaus in August of 1826. In an article dated 22 August 1826 *Kurjer Warszawski* [The Warsaw Courier] reported that:

> A letter received recently from the Silesian town of Kudowa (two miles from Reinertz) honorably reports about the young Polish artist, Fryderyk Chopin who, on advice of Warsaw Doctors, has been in Reinertz for a while in order to restore his health. When a few children became orphaned after their father's death there, Mr. Chopin, encouraged by persons who were familiar with his talent, gave two concerts for the aforementioned children, which gave him much glory and brought the unfortunates much succor. (This youth has been heard in piano performances in Warsaw on many occasions and has always received the most deserved appreciation of his beautiful talent.)[11]

Another trip, this time to Berlin in 1828, with a family friend, Professor Jarocki, provided Chopin with the opportunities to hear several concerts and operas. He rubbed shoulders with such musical celebrities as Gaspare Spontini (1774-1851) and the young Felix Mendelssohn, whom Chopin befriended later. When he returned to Warsaw, he was given a small studio on the top floor of the building where his family lived, where he was able to devote all of his time to music. A series of concerts given in Warsaw in 1828 by Johann Nepomuk Hummel (1778-1837), a virtuoso pianist-composer and a student of Mozart, inspired the young Chopin to revise and recast his Opus 1 *Rondeau*. Similarly, Niccolò Paganini's ten concert series in Warsaw between late May and July 1829 were echoed in some of the Op. 10 Etudes that were written around that time. After three years of studying with Elsner, the teacher's final report in July 1829 was brief: "Chopin, Fryderyk (third year student); outstanding abilities, *musical genius*, etc."[12]

Before Chopin finished his studies in Warsaw, his father petitioned the Minister for Public Instruction for an annual grant that would enable Frederic to "visit foreign countries, especially Germany, Italy, and France, so as to form himself upon the best models."[13] Although the request was turned down, Chopin's family provided him with enough funds to travel to Vienna during the summer of 1829. He appeared in the famous Kärntnertor Theatre on 11 August and again on the 18th, performing his *Don Giovanni Variations* on the first program and the *Rondo à la Krakowiak* on the second. Both concerts also featured some improvisations and were quite favorably received. Chopin was also able to meet many local musicians, including Carl Czerny (1791-1857) who was a pupil of Beethoven and a prolific author of piano etudes. He travelled back to Poland by way of Prague and Dresden, returning to Warsaw by mid-September.

Highlights of the fall season included Chopin's visit with the Radziwiłł family at their estate in Antonin and the completion of the F minor Piano Concerto, which was premiered at the National Theatre in Warsaw on 17 March 1830. The success of this concert, where Chopin also performed his *Fantasia on National Airs*, Op. 13, was such that a second concert had to be given on 22 March to accommodate the overflow audience. On this occasion Chopin performed both the F minor Concerto and *Rondo à la Krakowiak*. Both concerts were sold out and

Figure 9: Eliza Radziwiłł: Frederic Chopin at the piano. A pencil drawing in a diary kept by Eliza Radziwiłł during the years 1826-1831, dated 1826 [1829?]. Collection of the Frederic Chopin Museum at the Frederic Chopin National Institute. Owned by the Frederic Chopin Society, M/230. Used by permission

local press was ecstatic. Chopin immediately set out to write another piano concerto and—having just fallen in love with a young singer, Konstancja Gładkowska—he also wrote some beautifully tender music, including the Op. 9 and Op. 15 Nocturnes, and the E major Etude from Op. 10.

The late spring and summer of 1830 featured a visit of the Russian tsar in Warsaw and the atmosphere in Poland's formal capital was tense. During the summer months Chopin visited the country, calling on his birthplace of Żelazowa Wola for the last time. Back in Warsaw in September, he rehearsed his E minor Piano Concerto and gave his last concert in Warsaw on 11 October 1830. This time even Chopin admitted to being pleased with his performance, reporting a day later in a letter to his friend, Tytus Wojciechowski, "… I was not a bit, not a bit nervous, and played the way I play when I'm alone, and it went well."[14] After the Concerto Chopin also performed his *Fantasia* Op. 13:

This time the last mazurka elicited big applause, after which—the usual farce—I was called up. No one hissed, and I had to bow 4 times; […] I don't know how things would have gone yesterday if Soliwa had not taken my scores home with him, read them and conducted so that I could not rush as if I would break my neck. But he managed so well to hold us all that, I assure you, I never succeeded in playing so comfortably with the orchestra.[15]

Only three weeks later Chopin left Poland for Vienna. On the outskirts of Warsaw he was serenaded by a group of students led by Józef Elsner who wrote a short farewell cantata scored for the male choir and guitar. Stopping briefly in Breslau, Dresden, and Prague, Chopin reached Vienna on 22 November 1830. Only a week later

Figure 10: Antonin, the hunting lodge of Antoni Radziwiłł in the hamlet of Antonin. A contemporary photograph by Ewa Sławińska-Dahlig. Photo Collection of the Frederic Chopin National Institute. Used by permission

the anti-Russian uprising broke out in Warsaw. Tytus Wojciechowski, who had travelled to Vienna with Chopin, decided to return to Poland at once and join in the patriotic effort. Worried about the safety of his family, Chopin also considered going back to Warsaw. He was torn between being with his relatives in Poland and continuing to develop his career abroad. Plagued with doubts about the future he spent several difficult months in Vienna. His exile abroad had just begun.

———

Just like Chopin's visit in Berlin in 1828 to sample musical life there, Paderewski's first voyage abroad in 1882 also had Berlin as its destination.[16] Paderewski must have reached the same conclusion as Chopin regarding the somewhat provincial nature of musical life in Warsaw. As a result, venturing abroad for further study—"to form himself upon the best models," exactly as Chopin's father had put it earlier—seemed to be Paderewski's only logical choice. Even before he left for Berlin, Paderewski was offered a teaching post at the Warsaw Musical Institute. It was an offer worth considering, especially since his personal life had undergone a transformation:

And now we come to a great event in my life. I think I shall have to say it very simply—I fell in love. I was only twenty at that time and in spite of the uncertainty of the future, I married. I wanted a home, a personal life of my own—a place and some one that belonged to me. I married in 1880 Antonina Korsak—a young girl who was a student at the Warsaw Conservatory. I had a little home of my own at last and I was happy—but it was a short happiness. a year later my wife died, leaving me alone with our child, a son. I had lived through a brief—a beautiful—experience. Even at twenty, one can plumb the heights and depths and feel the pain and mystery of life. I now faced another change—I must go forward alone. […] I realized very keenly that there was no future for me there in Warsaw except as a teacher, and so I determined to go to Berlin. I left my child with his grandmother, the mother of my wife, and went directly to Friedrich Kiel, a very famous teacher of that time, to study composition.[17]

Since becoming a professional musician was foremost on Paderewski's mind, he left his family and friends in Warsaw and set out for Berlin. He was twenty-two years old when he reached the German capital in January 1882. He remained there for about a year, occasionally going back to Poland to visit and perform. During the first half of 1884 Paderewski was again in Berlin, studying composition this time with Heinrich Urban. Being a Polish patriot in Berlin was rather difficult:

I was a Pole and very much alone. As I remember it, there were few Polish students there at that time. The Germans were not at all sympathetic to me. That was a time of great persecution of the Poles in Germany and I felt it constantly and deeply. Even in that charming family of my kind publisher, Mr. Bock, I sometimes had to hear very cutting and bitter remarks about my country. And I disliked Berlin very, very much on that account. There were certain political regulations which made me feel rather disgusted with these people and their system. For example, of all the foreign newspapers, only the Polish were prohibited. There was no sale of them at the railway stations (the stations always have foreign papers). Some individuals were very nice, very civilized, but the entire atmosphere was positively antagonistic to Poland.[18]

Nonetheless, the Berlin period was important for Paderewski as he was able to meet a number of prominent musicians and befriend a good many of them. Maurycy Moszkowski (1854-1925), a brilliant Polish pianist and composer born in Breslau who settled in Berlin, was the first of Paderewski's local acquaintances who became a lifelong friend. Moszkowski introduced Paderewski to the Bock publishing family and their salon, frequented by such stellar musicians as violinists Joseph Joachim (1831-1907) and Pablo de Sarasate (1844-1908), pianist Eugène d'Albert (1864-1932), and composer Richard Strauss (1864-1949).

Closer to home, one of Paderewski's most important friendships was with the Górski family. Władysław Górski (1846-1915) was a Polish violinist who graduated from the Institute of Music in Warsaw and then studied composition with Ferdinand Kiel in Berlin. He concertized throughout Europe, and his salon in Warsaw was a gathering place for the musical elite. Górski was married to Baroness Helena von Rosen (1856-1934), who took great interest in the young Paderewski as he frequently performed chamber music concerts with her husband. Through the Górskis Paderewski met the most famous Polish actress, Helena Modrzejewska (1840-1909).[19]

After her spectacular career on stages in Kraków and Warsaw, Modjeska conquered the United States and England, specializing in Shakespearean roles. Modjeska met

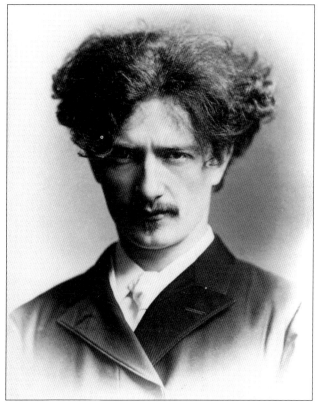

Figure 11: Paderewski in Berlin, mid-1880s. The Paso Robles Collection, Polish Music Center, USC.

Paderewski during the summer season in the mountain resort of Zakopane, where he appeared in concert with Władysław Górski. Modjeska remembered the meeting vividly:

In 1884-1885 we stayed in Poland and England. We first went to Paris to visit my son, then to Zakopane in the Tatra Mountains, where we had built a villa... As we neared Zakopane, many friends and mountaineers met and greeted us with cheers. We stopped our wagon, and a long while was spent in the exchanging words of joy, embracing and kissing. While we were thus engaged, another wagon came up to us and stopped. I heard a sweet voice from the depth of it, calling, "Madame Helena! How do you do?" And a beautiful face of Madame Górska (the present Madame Paderewska), appeared between the white canvass of the wagon. New greetings, new exclamations.

The beautiful creature, whose name is also Helena, looked at me with her wistful eyes and said: "I envy your going to Zakopane; you are going to meet one of the most extraordinary young men you ever met." Then she sighed and said, "And I must go away." "I must," she repeated, lower. "Good-by," and she parted.

The very next day Dr. Tytus Chałubiński introduced us to a frail-looking young man of twenty-one, saying, "I want you to know and love Ignace Paderewski, our second Chopin," and then with a look of a loving father he squeezed the young man's hand.

At the piano, Paderewski's head, with its aureole of profuse golden hair and delicate, almost feminine features, looked like one of Botticelli's or Fran Angelico's angels, and he seemed so deeply wrapped up in his music that this intensity was almost hypnotic. He also phrased with so much clearness and meaning that his playing made an effect of something new and unconventional…

In private life he was witty, alert, kind-hearted, always interesting, always having a ready answer… He used to come often to our villa, and it was impossible to keep him away from the piano. Sometimes he played long after midnight, and had to be taken from the instrument by force when the refreshments were announced.

We had many chats, and I advised him to appear in public. I knew he would make a name and a fortune. His poetic face, combined with his genius, was bound to produce brilliant results. He hesitated, but finally made up his mind to go to Vienna and study with Leschetizky. At the end of summer, after leaving Zakopane, he gave a concert at which I had the pleasure of reciting. Then he departed for Vienna.[20]

Modjeska seems to be quite modest in describing her role in Paderewski's musical development. Whilst in 1884 her protégé was only a young and promising pianist-composer, she was already an internationally famous actress.[20] By suggesting joint appearances on the soirées of music and poetry in Kraków in October of 1884, she was instrumental in raising funds for Paderewski's studies in Vienna.[21]

Paderewski spent the better part of the next three years in the capital of Austria-Hungary, studying with Teodor Leschetizky, one of the most famous piano pedagogues of the time. At first Leschetizky thought that his new student—aged twenty-four, already a composer and performer of some reputation—was too old to study piano with a view of becoming a performing virtuoso. Paderewski however, was determined to follow though a rigorous course of exercises and basic technique development:

Although my student life was a happy one in Vienna, I worked very hard. I had absolutely no relaxation—it was work, work, work. […] I used to practice seven hours a day during all that stay in Vienna—and my recreation and amusement? Well, my lessons with Leschetizky filled my horizon, for that was study and recreation and inspiration at the same time. […] I lived then in two very humble rooms not far from Leschetizky's villa. For many years I had them, and into these little rooms were crowded all the memories of my struggles and disappointments—the years of hard, unceasing work—my first debut in Vienna and my first composition of a large form (my Concerto was written there, you know). […] From them I went forth to meet life, and out of that sentiment I was very much attached to them and kept them for many years after I became a successful pianist.[22]

Gradually, success and recognition came Paderewski's way. He befriended Johannes Brahms (1833-1897), the most important musician living in Vienna, who expressed appreciation of Paderewski's compositions and was amiably disposed towards the young Polish pianist. In contrast to Berlin, Paderewski found Vienna a wonderful, lively, and deeply musical place:

There was a stamp of officialdom in everything in Berlin, owing to that military system and the strong iron hand of the Government. In Vienna there was much more freedom, much more possibility for the display of personalities. There was a charm and sparkle in the very atmosphere there—a charm in the people, charm in everything! Vienna was a city of charm, and I am still very fond of it. It is a city of my heart. […] There was much splendid music, the orchestra, the Philharmonic, being one of the finest in the world (much finer than Berlin Philharmonic).[23]

Paderewski's intense studies with Leschetizky—broken only by a year-long professorship at the Music Conservatoire in Strasbourg and a few concert appearances in Warsaw—culminated in his highly successful March 1888 debut at the Salle Érard in Paris. Within the next two weeks Paderewski followed up by presenting two programs devoted exclusively to his own compositions (Władysław Górski appeared with him in Paderewski's Sonata for Violin and Piano), and shortly thereafter he performed Saint-Saëns' Fourth Piano Concerto with the Lamoureux Orchestra. His career as concert pianist and world-famous virtuoso had finally taken off.

1 A member of the Iwanowski family, Zygmunt (1875-1944) was also born in Kuryłówka. He was a painter of portraits, nudes, and cityscapes who came to America in 1902 and settled in Mountainside, NJ. There is no information on any contacts between Paderewski and Iwanowski, although the latter certainly must have heard of Paderewski's life and career.

2 See *Memoirs* by Paderewski and Lawton, p. 3

3 Throughout his life Paderewski had only very limited contact with his stepbrother and stepsister and, to the extent it can be ascertained, it occurred mainly during the 1920s and the 1930s. Paderewski's stepbrother, Józef, presumed killed in the early days of World War II, had surfaced in Poland in 1946. Poland's Communist Government tried to lay a claim to Paderewski's estate on behalf of his stepbrother, and employed a New York law firm to represent the claim in court. In the 1930s Paderewski's stepsister, Maria, was known to be living in utter poverty in Soviet Russia. She had suffered repeated interrogations by secret police and died some time in the early 1950s. The Hoover Institution Library Archives has a copy of a letter from Paderewski to Maxim Maximovich Litvinov (1876-1951), the Russian ambassador to the League of Nations from 1934-1938. Paderewski wrote on behalf of Maria, who lived near Zhitomir in the Ukraine, asking for help in allowing her to immigrate to Poland. Nothing more is known of the outcome of this petition.

4 See excerpt form diaries of Alexandra Tańska, quoted in Arthur Hedley's *Chopin*, p. 21

5 See *Memoirs* by Paderewski and Lawton, p. 17

6 Ibid., p. 15

7 Ibid., p. 27

8 Ibid., p. 38

9 See Chopin's Letters, pp. 28-29

10 See Chopin's Letters, p. 30

11 See *Tam, gdzie Chopin chodził na pół czarnej...* [Where Chopin had his espresso...], p. 31. (Translated by the author)

12 See Arthur Hedley, *Chopin*, p. 31

13 Ibid., p. 30

14 See Chopin's Letters, p. 113

15 Ibid., p. 114

16 Until that time Paderewski had performed only in either Russian-occupied territories of Poland, or Russia.

17 From *Memoirs* by Paderewski and Lawton, pp. 56-57

18 Ibid., p. 62

19 Modrzejewska used the anglicized spelling of her name, "Modjeska," when performing outside of Poland.

20 From *Memories and Impressions* by Helena Modjeska, pp. 464-468

21 Paderewski was already known in the mountain resort of Zakopane, as he had performed there in the late 1870s and early 1880s with violinist Władysław Górski. Górski's wife, Helena, later divorced her first husband in order to marry Paderewski. For more details see the essay by Teresa Chylińska, *Niewykorzystana szansa, czyli dzieje muzyczne Zakopanego* [The Lost Chance, or the Musical History of Zakopane] in a book, *Zakopane—czterysta lat dziejów* [Zakopane—Four Hundred Years of History], published by Krajowa Agencja Wydawnicza, Kraków, 1991.

22 From *Memories and Impressions* by Helena Modjeska, pp. 466-468

23 From *Memoirs* by Paderewski and Lawton, pp. 88-89

23 Ibid., p. 93

Figure 12: Chopin's birthplace in a period lithograph. Reproduced in H. Opieński, *Chopin*. Polish Music Center Archives, USC

~ CHAPTER THREE ~

WARSAW, VIENNA, PARIS, AND BEYOND

For Chopin and Paderewski, the road to recognition led from Warsaw through Vienna to Paris. For both artists each phase of their journey along that same route marked an important stage in the development of their careers, and the degree to which the trajectories of their careers were in effect quite similar is indeed remarkable.

As original and as innovative Chopin's music is in the history of music, the origins of his compositions can still be traced back to keyboard compositions written by some of his immediate predecessors. This is especially true of Chopin's early creations, mostly the Polonaises and a few Mazurkas that Chopin began to write even before he reached his teenage years.[1] The artistic models for Chopin's early opus were Polish and European keyboard virtuosos and composers, who had begun to explore several new genres that Chopin later perfected and transformed.

Prince Michał Kleofas Ogiński (1764-1833) was a prominent politician and composer who wrote a number of short keyboard works, among which the most interesting are various Polish dances, including Polonaises. One of them, titled *Pożegnanie Ojczyzny* [Farewell to the Homeland], became very popular during Ogiński's life and it remains well-known to this day. His music is often lyrical and shows little virtuosity but its deeply personal note represents the earliest manifestations of Romanticism in Polish music:

Whenever during my peregrinations perchance I found a piano, I automatically sat down and drew from it sad, heartrending, sometimes even agitated sounds, as if inspired by some visions.[2]

Ogiński transformed the generic form of the Polonaise (as written by Bach, Telemann, Handel or Mozart) into a national dance with specifically Polish characteristics. After an active life in Polish, Russian and French politics, Ogiński spent the last decade of his life in exile in Florence, Italy.

Maria Szymanowska (1789-1831) was one of the first women virtuosos and composers of note in the early decades of the Romantic era. Szymanowska's opus includes many piano miniatures, including Nocturnes, Etudes, Mazurkas, Caprices and Fantasias. They became very popular in her lifetime and, judging by Chopin's lifelong dedication to the exploration of the same genres, Szymanowska's music must have influenced him to some extent. After studying composition with Franciszek Lessel, Karol Kurpiński and Józef Elsner (who later taught Chopin), Szymanowska first appeared in Warsaw and Paris in 1810 and then went on to concertize extensively across Europe, performing her repertoire from memory which was quite rare at that time. It is likely that the seventeen-year old Chopin attended Szymanowska's 1827 Warsaw performance, as he rarely missed any important music event in his hometown. In addition, a good deal of Szymanowska's music was published by mid 1820s and it is almost certain that Chopin was aware of it.[3] Szymanowska was one of the most widely-known and celebrated Polish artists, whose close friends included poets Johann Wolfgang von Goethe (1749-1832), Adam Mickiewicz (1798-1855), and Alexander Pushkin (1799-1837). Two great piano virtuosos and famous composers of the early Romantic *style brillant*— Johann Nepomuk Hummel and John Field (1782-1837)—also belonged to Szymanowska's circle of friends. Both Hummel and Field concertized extensively in Poland and Russia. Chopin heard Hummel in Warsaw and, just like Szymanowska before him, had several of Hummel's and Field's compositions in his repertoire. Chopin was on friendly terms with Hummel and his son, and reported to his family from Vienna in December of 1830:

A propos of painting: yesterday morning Hummel came to me with his son; he is finishing my portrait; it's so like that it couldn't be better. I am sitting on a stool, in a dressing-gown, with an inspired expression of I don't know what. Pencil, or rather chalk, looks like an engraving; size for a folder. Old Hummel is kindness itself. As he is friendly with Duport, formerly a famous dancer and the entrepreneur of the Kärthnerthor theatre, he introduced me to him yesterday.[4]

John Field—another early influence on Chopin's musical development—was the first composer to write Nocturnes for piano, a genre which Chopin transcended and turned into a remarkable avenue for some his most personal music. Although Chopin's early Polonaises and Mazurkas come from the tradition of similar works by Ogiński and Szymanowska, they already exhibit more sophisticated pianistic textures and harmonies. On the other hand Chopin's youthful Rondos, Variations, chamber music and works for piano and orchestra owe much to the *style brillant* of works by Field or Hummel, whose music bridged the Classical and the Romantic era.

———————

Like Chopin, Paderewski began to compose in his teenage years. His first attempt, the *Valse mignonne* dedicated to his piano teacher Gustaw Roguski, dates from 1876 when Paderewski was sixteen. His other piano juvenilia—published many years later—include an *Impromptu*, a Suite in E-flat major, and a programmatic *Powódź* [The Flood]. None of these works betray much individuality or an attempt at forging new paths in music. Even when we consider Paderewski's works for piano which were published at the onset of his musical career in the early 1880s—*Zwei Klavierstücke*, *Trois Morceaux*, *Elegie*, the two sets of *Danses polonaises*, and collections like *Chants du voyageur*,

Album de mai, or the *Tatra Album*—we find that they are predominantly short salon pieces containing a nice turn of phrase here and there, but are otherwise quite unremarkable. One of the reasons for their lack of originality may be that after Chopin's death in 1849 there were only a few Polish composers of note on Poland's musical scene who could serve as models for Paderewski. The most prominent of them—Stanisław Moniuszko (1819-1872)—was primarily a composer of vocal music, author of several popular operas and numerous songs with piano accompaniment, as well as a large body of religious music.[5] Moniuszko's compositions for solo piano are quite negligible and certainly cannot be classified as groundbreaking. As such they could hardly inspire the younger generation of Polish musicians. This situation did not really change until the end of the nineteenth century when a few more promising talents emerged. The first to build upon Chopin's legacy and carry it into a new realm of music was Juliusz Zarębski (1854-1885), a brilliant pianist and a fascinating composer who studied with Liszt and wrote some very interesting and harmonically advanced piano music. His death of tuberculosis at the age of thirty-one and the subsequent obscurity of his opus made it unlikely that during his formative years Paderewski had known any of Zarębski's compositions. Karol Szymanowski (1882-1937), regarded as the most important Polish composer after Chopin, did not begin to publish music until the early 1900s, just when Paderewski's career as composer was ending.

The important and notable exceptions in Paderewski's catalogue of early compositions are his Sonata for Violin and Piano, Op. 13 (published in 1885), *Vier Lieder*, Op. 7 (a cycle of four songs for voice and piano published in 1886), two cycles of piano pieces: the *Humoresques de concert*, Op. 14 (published in 1887) and the *Miscellanea*, Op. 16 (published in 1888-1894), as well as his Piano Concerto in A minor, Op. 17 (published in 1890). In his solo piano works Paderewski followed the style of Romantic miniatures written by such German composers as Felix Mendelssohn and Robert Schumann. Mendelssohn's numerous *Songs without Words* for piano and Schumann's shorter piano compositions (*Fantasiestücke*, *Nachtstücke*, *Waldszenen*) likely served as inspiration for young Paderewski as he always retained these compositions in his repertoire.

Some of Paderewski's compositions published in the late 1880s achieved spectacular popularity: the Op. 14 *Menuet*, for example, remains Paderewski's musical trademark to this day. Although less well known, Paderewski's other solo piano pieces (like the *Cracovienne fantastique* from Op. 14 or the two *Legends* and the *Nocturne* from Op. 16) are also beautifully written and certainly merit their inclusion in the concert repertoire of every pianist. Paderewski's Piano Concerto—written during his studies in Vienna and dedicated to his teacher, Leschetizky—is also an excellent and very effective work. Its attractive piano part and skillfully handled orchestration attracted the famous German conductor, Hans Richter to premiere this composition in Vienna. The soloist for that occasion was Annette Essipov, Leschetizky's wife and a close friend of Paderewski.[6] The success of his Concerto in Vienna and the great triumph of Paderewski's debut concerts in Paris in 1888 finally established him as a pianist and composer of international standing.

It was through their concerts—first in Vienna, then in Paris—that Chopin and Paderewski were introduced to the international public. Chopin's journey to Paris was taken in several stages and began after a long second visit in Vienna, which began in late November of 1830. As the option of returning to Poland (where anti-Russian revolt was in progress) was no longer viable, after prevaricating for several months about where to go next, Chopin finally set out for Paris in early summer of 1831. Since he was legally a Russian subject, the tsarist police did not wish Chopin to join other Polish émigrés and political conspirators in Paris. As a result, Chopin's passport was valid for travel "to London via Paris." By August 1831 Chopin reached Germany, and on the 28th performed his E minor Concerto and *Fantasie on Polish Airs* in Munich. By early September the news of the fall of Warsaw to the Russian army had reached him in Stuttgart. Chopin's frantic, practically incoherent reaction scribbled in his notebook shows how deeply he was affected by the brutal suppression of the Polish uprising by the Russian army. He finally reached Paris in October of 1831 and rented a modest top-floor flat at 27, Boulevard Poissonière.

Chopin's new lodgings had beautiful views of Montmartre and the Paris Conservatoire was only a block away on the Rue Bergère. A year later Chopin moved to a second floor apartment at 4, Cité-Bergère, even closer to the Conservatoire, and then relocated to a very fashionable address of Chausée d'Antin in the Second Arrondissement. He lived there from 1833 until 1839, first at no. 5, later at no. 38.[7]

At the time of Chopin's arrival in Paris, the French capital had been transformed by the July 1830 Revolution that ended the reign of Charles X who was forced into exile in England. Louis-Philippe, "the Citizen-King" became the last King of France in August of 1831, thanks to the vote of the Chamber of Deputies who supported the new king's liberal policies. Just as in politics, the world of arts and music was undergoing a profound change. A new generation of musicians, writers, painters, philosophers and architects came to the fore after being inspired by the political upheaval that began with the Napoleonic Wars and led to the 1830 Revolution. Names like Hugo, Balzac, Stendhal, de Vigny, Lamartine, de Musset, Géricault, Delacroix, or Ingres are synonymous with the blossoming of the French

Figure 13: Paris in the mid-1840s with a view of the Chausée d'Antin. Polish Music Center Archives.

Romantic art tradition. Liszt and Berlioz with their revolutionary ideas in music transformed the institution of public and private concerts. After the deaths of Beethoven and Schubert in the late 1820s, Vienna began to cede its musical preeminence to Paris, where the most important musical personalities of the Romantic era had gravitated—Franz Liszt, Hector Berlioz, Gioachino Rossini, Luigi Cherubini, Maria Malibran, Giuditta Pasta, Ferdinando Paer, and Friedrich Kalkbrenner, among many others. Most of the musicians from this exclusive sphere as well as a number of friends from the highest echelons of the Polish émigré society heard

Chopin's Parisian debut on 26 February 1832 at Salle Pleyel on Rue Cadet. Billed as a "Grand Vocal and Instrumental Concert," the program included Beethoven's Op. 29 Quintet, Chopin's solo performance of his F minor Piano Concerto, Kalkbrenner's *Grand Polonaise with Introduction and March* for six pianos, and Chopin's *Don Giovanni Variations* which closed the evening.[8] Franz Liszt and Felix Mendelssohn were present and there was no doubt that the audience of Chopin's peers was completely astounded. Musicologist, professor of Paris Conservatoire and a noted music critic, François-Joseph Fétis, wrote about Chopin in the *Revue musicale*:

37

[...] Here is a young man who, surrendering himself to his natural impressions and taking no model, has found, if not a complete renewal of piano music, at least a part that which we have long sought in vain, namely an abundance of original ideas of a kind to be found nowhere else... I find in Mr. Chopin's inspirations the signs of a renewal of forms which may henceforth exercise considerable influence upon this branch of the art.[9]

Three years later, Chopin's magical debut was still fresh in the memory of his friend, Felix Mendelssohn, who wrote:

There is something so thoroughly original and at the same time so very masterly in his piano playing that he may be called a really perfect virtuoso. I was glad to be once again with a thorough musician, not one of those half-virtuosos and half-classics who would like to combine in music the honours of virtue and the pleasure of vice, but one who has his own perfect and clearly defined style.[10]

In the meantime, Chopin performed in Paris once again, this time at a charity concert held on 20 May 1832 at the Conservatoire. He played only the first movement of his F minor concerto and on this occasion was accompanied by an orchestra. Unfortunately the piano Chopin used had a small tone and his performance did not impress his audience as much as his February debut. Temporarily, Chopin's prospects for a successful future as a performing virtuoso and composer in Paris suddenly seemed less certain. A more favorable turn of fortune came when Prince Radziwiłł introduced Chopin to the Parisian branch of the Rothschild family. Shortly thereafter Chopin became a sought-after piano teacher for a number of aristocratic pupils and his financial situation improved dramatically. The most exclusive salons of Paris opened their doors and Chopin's excitement at his sudden rise to the top of Parisian society is quite palpable in this 1832 letter to his childhood friend, Dominik Dziewanowski:

I have got into the highest society; I sit with ambassadors, princes, ministers; and even don't know how it came about, because I did not try for it. It is a most necessary thing for me, because good taste is supposed to depend on it. At once you have a bigger talent if you have been heard at the English or Austrian embassy; you play better if princess Vaudemont (the last of the old Montmorency family) was your protector; I can't say is, because the woman died a week ago. [...] One proof of respect is that even people with huge reputations dedicate their compositions to me before I do so to them [...] in a word, finished artists take lessons from me and couple my name with that of Field. In short, if I were still stupider than I am, I should think myself at the apex of my career; yet I know how much I still lack, to reach perfection; I see it the more clearly now that I live only among first-rank artists and know what each one of them lacks.[11]

Having joined the artistic elite of Paris, for the next several years Chopin lived a comfortable life in an elegantly-furnished apartment with a private carriage at his disposal, a manservant

Figure 14: "Place de la Concorde" from a series of lithographs depicting Paris in 1860. Private collection. Used by permission. All rights reserved.

on duty, and a great selection of impeccable attire for any time of day or night. He gave several lessons per day and was quite content to perform in public only sporadically. In April of 1833 he was heard in another multi-piano concert extravaganza with his friend Franz Liszt and, at the end of that year, joined Liszt and another pianist friend, Ferdinand Hiller, in concert of Bach's Concerto for Three Keyboards at the Conservatoire. In April of 1835 he played at the Italian Opera for a benefit of Polish political refugees in Paris, but his performance of the E minor Concerto was only politely received. A few weeks later he was heard on the Paris Conservatoire concert series with the resident orchestra in his *Andante spianato and*

Figure 15: "Palais-Royal" from a series of lithographs depicting Paris in 1860. Private collection. Used by permission.

Grand Polonaise, Op. 22. It was a very successful concert but, as history would have it, it was Chopin's last major venue appearance in Paris. Afterwards he decided to retire from large-scale public events and perform only for small and intimate gatherings. The three concerts that Chopin gave in Paris in 1841, 1842, and 1848, were semi-private, invitation-only affairs, given for the carefully selected audiences of fewer than three hundred listeners each.

———————

Paderewski's Parisian debut concert at Salle Érard on 3 March 1888 marks the date of his triumphant entry on the international concert scene. Many years later, when he was working on his *Memoirs*, Paderewski candidly admitted that the public did not immediately warm up to his playing until the middle of his Salle Érard program. However, just like Chopin's debut in Paris over half a century earlier, Paderewski's recital was attended by the musical elite and a number of Polish aristocrats. His "brilliant audience," was there to hear him because,

[…] there was quite a large colony of Polish people in Paris at that time, aristocrats, highly cultured and very musical, and they all attended this concert and brought their friends of the French aristocracy. That explains the "brilliance" of the audience. I was unknown. It was my nationality that helped me a great deal in gathering together these distinguished folk. Besides the notables already mentioned, there were many prominent French people present, foreigners and some famous musicians as well. Tchaikovsky, the great Russian composer, who was then in Paris, was there. Then there were the two famous orchestra conductors—Colonne and Lamoureux, and of course Madame Essipoff and my dear friend, Princess Brancovan, and Madame Trélat, Madame Dubois, the last pupil of Chopin, and so many others. In fact, most of the prominent musicians of the time were there. The hall was crowded. They were so enthusiastic that I had to play for another hour after the concert. It was all very exciting and I think I may say it was really a tremendous success. I could hardly believe it—after all my doubts and fears.[12]

The immense success of Paderewski's performance immediately led to other engagements and to an instant (and shocking) realization that this was a long awaited success that came too soon! Although Paderewski was twenty-eight, he was still at the beginning of his pianistic career and his recital repertoire was quite small. Since he did not expect such a remarkable reaction from his audience, he planned on playing only one concert in Paris. Suddenly there were numerous offers of additional solo recitals and appearances with orchestras that had to be accepted.

There was only one thing to do. So I had to prepare very quickly a second program. I began to work immediately. There was no other way. I was three weeks working on the second program. How did I ever do it! Even now I cannot tell how. It was colossal. The first program took eight months. Imagine what one could do in three weeks! But—I did the impossible! I prepared it somehow. It was not perfect academically, but I got it into shape. I met the challenge with my towering ambition and youth—and youth is a tremendous force. […] There is nothing more terrible than to meet a good success for which one is not ready or ripe. It is an agony.[13]

Afterwards Paderewski returned to Leschetizky in Vienna to work on polishing up his concert repertoire. His recital at the Bösendorfer Hall in Vienna in 1889 was another great and immediate success with the public. The critical acclaim was unanimous and with such an unequivocal blessing Paderewski felt much reassured. He returned to Paris for more recitals and gradually began to accept engagements from all across Europe. For the time being he decided to settle in Paris, but was still conscious of his shortcomings as a pianist with limited repertoire:

I decided to make Paris my headquarters and took a small apartment in the Avenue Victor Hugo—a very small and modest one it was, but still I had to get my roots, so to speak, into the ground. That little apartment was very dear to my heart. Just as the two little rooms in Vienna, it became a part of my life and, as in Vienna, I kept the Paris apartment for many years, until 1906 in fact. It was all connected with my work, a little world of my own—a world of work, of increasing work, a work that never stopped. And I know as absolutely today as then that I was always struggling for perfection, pushing on to that ever-receding, faraway peak of attainment. My greatest anxiety in those years was learning new programs and giving them to the audiences.[14]

During the early years of his life in Paris, Paderewski befriended a number of prominent musicians, including the operatic composer, Charles Gounod (1818-1893), and the brilliant piano virtuoso and composer, Camille Saint-Saëns (1835-1921). Shortly after his debut in Paris, Paderewski visited Saint-Saëns at home to play for him the recently completed Piano Concerto. Uncertain of how it might be received by his peers or the public, Paderewski was relieved to hear his older colleague's resounding recommendation:

You may play it whenever you like. It will please the people. It's quite ready. You needn't be afraid of it, I assure you.[15]

Besides making friends among the musicians, Paderewski—just like Chopin before him—also entered the aristocratic *beau monde* of Paris. Madame Camille Dubois, the last pupil of Chopin, became one of Paderewski's most influential acquaintances after hearing the young Polish pianist's Parisian debut. Her salon attracted the *crème de la crème* of French society and Paderewski soon joined that circle as well. Madame Dubois' scores of Chopin's music, which were used in her lessons during the period 1843-1848, contain numerous pencil markings in Chopin's hand.[16] After Chopin's death, she became one of his most ardent and faithful disciples, who scrupulously guarded the performing tradition of Chopin's compositions. She shared her insights on interpreting Chopin's music with successive generations of pianists who came to her salon, including Paderewski:

I heard from her certain interesting remarks as they were made by the great Master himself, and I cannot deny that I derived some benefit from them, even at second hand. She told me many things of interest. I remember once when I was playing the 17th Prelude of Chopin, Madame Dubois said that Chopin himself used to play that bass note in the final section (in spite of playing everything else *diminuendo*) with great strength. He always *struck* that note in the same way and with the *same* strength, because of the meaning attached to it. [...] The idea of that Prelude is based on the sound of an old clock in the castle which strikes the *eleventh* hour.[17]

London was the next major city to be conquered by Paderewski. His success in England did not come immediately, since the first two of his recitals in St. James's Hall in May of 1890 were not sold out. But a generally favorable review in *The Times* resulted in the third recital to be a sold-out event. It was followed by appearances with orchestras in London, Manchester, and Liverpool and many more recitals throughout the British Isles. Interestingly, in a large measure Paderewski retraced Chopin's 1848 tour of England that—in Chopin's case—included several private performances in London (including a recital for the Queen, Prince Albert, Duke of Wellington, and about eighty other distinguished guests), and an extended visit to Scotland, where Chopin's host was his Parisian pupil, Miss Jane Stirling. Forty years after Chopin's sojourn in England Paderewski became the second great Polish pianist to make the rounds of private salons of London where, just like Chopin, he was

well received and handsomely rewarded by the patrician families who soon became Paderewski's cordial friends.[18] These included such distinguished personalities as the family of the Duke of Portland, Lord Balfour, the Duchess of Argyll, and various members of the royal family, including Queen Victoria for whom Paderewski played on two occasions. Paderewski's contacts in London proved extremely important during World War I when he became active in politics and worked for the cause of Poland's independence.

During the early years of his career, Paderewski also concertized throughout Germany. With the exception of Berlin, where his performance was sabotaged by the orchestra and tendentiously reviewed by the press, Paderewski's appearances during the 1890-1891 Season in Germany were very successful. After establishing himself as an artist in Europe, the next big step in Paderewski's career was his first tour of America.

Paderewski's debut in the United States took place on 17 November 1891, at the Music Hall (later renamed Carnegie Hall) with the New York Symphony Orchestra conducted by Walter Damrosch (1862-1950). His program included the Second Piano Concerto of Saint-

Saëns, a group of Chopin solo works, and Paderewski's own Piano Concerto in A minor. Over one hundred concerts and four and a half months later, Paderewski was back in New York to settle accounts with his sponsors, Steinway & Sons, and sign contracts for his 1892 tour.[19] The triumphant concert reviews throughout the United States set the tone for all of Paderewski's subsequent North American tours. His first visit in America brought Paderewski $100,000, an amazing and still very impressive figure, prompting the *Boston Globe* reporter to observe that "… if he continues gathering in the coin of the realm as he has done this year, there will not be much money left in the country."[20] On 29 March 1892 Paderewski sailed for Europe from New York no doubt longing for a well-earned rest. His first American tour set a certain timetable in motion that would be adhered to in the following tours of the New World. Paderewski usually arrived in New York in late fall and, after playing in the major cities of the East Coast, he moved to the Midwest and South during the winter and early spring. By April or May he would be sailing back to Europe. There was, however, one more region of the United States to explore, the West Coast. At the end of the nineteenth century American territories west of the Rockies were still a vast area of mostly pristine wilderness, with a few cities in California—San Francisco, Los Angeles and San Diego—that were just becoming major metropolitan areas and centers of burgeoning commerce. The spirit of adventure and promise of striking it rich in almost any new enterprise brought waves of new settlers from all over the world to California's welcoming shores. New business and social elites were quickly getting established in bigger cities and cultural life was blossoming as well.

Paderewski's first concerts in California took place during his third American tour. His arrival on the West Coast was duly noted by the *Los Angeles Times* on 6 February 1896. The headline: "Paderewski Arrived—Travels in a Private Car with His Suite" was followed by these first impressions recorded by a local reporter:

The idol of the musical world, the great Polish pianist, Paderewski, arrived in his private car last evening, at the Arcade station, where he remained over night, leaving for San Diego this morning. At San Antonio, the last place at which he played, he was greeted by a splendid house, and another big audience is already assured at San Diego.

Paderewski, as he left his car last evening, accompanied by his managers, and saw the deputation of press representatives lying in wait for him, was apparently possessed with a desire to flee, but finally wheeled about and permitted himself to be introduced, greeting each with a cordial handshake. He was very weary with his long trip, but chatted pleasantly for a few minutes. His son, he said, he had left in Paris, as the cramped quarters and the long trip were too much for him.

Paderewski is charming in his manners and when conversing, his face lights up and a genial smile plays about his mouth. He is medium height and very slender built; his hair, which had been greatly exaggerated, and is but slightly longer than men ordinarily wear it, is a fluffy mass of a rich auburn shade. His private secretary, who was discovered in a trip through the private car, "Haslemere," declared that all his peculiarities have been extremely exaggerated and that he does not consume the enormous number of cigarettes he is said to. His car is very elegantly appointed and is stocked with everything to make life comfortable on a long journey. In the compartment nearest the front end of the car was a large leather trunk, marked "I.J.P" and an upright piano, upon which Paderewski plays in quiet hours and at rare intervals while the train is in motion. The piano manufacturers are said to pay him $150,000 a season to use only their pianos, and the young man who poses as private secretary is really their agent, who goes along to see that the contract is carried out. Two pianos are all the time upon the road, one in advance of the other, and Paderewski plays only upon these. He takes with him in his car, Messrs. Gorlitz and Frye, his managers, the private secretary, a butler and a valet.

The great pianist will arrive from San Diego Friday afternoon at 5 o'clock, and will play that evening and Saturday afternoon at the Los Angeles Theater.[21]

Figure 16: Paderewski (center) and his wife, Helena, inside his Pullman car during a US tour in the early 1920s. The Paso Robles Collection, Polish Music Center, USC.

and began to make recordings. His popularity rose steadily and he undoubtedly became the most famous artist of his era. Paderewski was a touring concert pianist almost to the end of his long life: his last stage appearances took place during his twentieth tour of the United States in 1939. Without a doubt he managed to realize his dream of becoming a famous virtuoso to an extent he certainly could not foresee when he first entered the concert stage of Salle Érard in Paris in 1888.

By the early 1900s Paderewski was roaming all corners of the earth and travelling with concerts to Australia and New Zealand. Later he visited South Africa and South America,

1 Chopin's first published composition was a Polonaise in G minor, written and published in 1817. During the same year he wrote the *Military March* and another Polonaise in B-flat major. The Polonaise in A-flat major, dedicated to Chopin's first teacher, Żywny, dates from 1821, and was followed by the Polonaise in G-sharp minor in 1822, a few Mazurkas, and a C minor Rondo, Op. 1 in 1825, then a set of *Écossaises* and the "Swiss Boy" Variations, in 1826.

2 See *Dzieje muzyki polskiej* [The History of Polish Music], Tadeusz Ochlewski, Ed., p., 64

3 See Sławomir Dobrzański, *Maria Szymanowska—Pianist and Composer*, p. 100

4 See Chopin's letters, p. 127

5 Moniuszko had a very modest view of his musical accomplishments, especially when compared to those of Chopin. In a December 1850 letter to Józef Sikorski, he stated, "If someone is stupid enough to find consolation in my existence after Chopin's death, it is not my fault; I have never placed myself next to any legitimate European celebrity, never mind Chopin for whom my admiration knows no bounds!!!"

6 For more details of the Concerto's premiere, see *Memoirs* by Paderewski and Lawton, pp. 120-121. Annette Essipoff was Leschetizky's wife from 1880 until 1891

7 See William G. Atwood, *Parisian Worlds of Frederic Chopin*, p. 16

8 See Arthur Hedley, *Chopin*, p. 57

9 Ibid., p. 58

10 Ibid., p. 61

11 See Chopin's letters, p. 168-169

12 See Paderewski and Lawton, *Memoirs*, p. 115-116

13 Ibid., p. 118

14 Ibid., p. 133

15 Ibid., p 137

16 See Eigeldinger, *Chopin: Pianist and Teacher*, p. 164

17 See Paderewski and Lawton, *Memoirs*, p 142

18 Chopin charged twenty guineas for his "at home" concerts in 1848. Paderewski in the early 1890s charged sixty guineas—apparently a prevailing rate at that time—for his private performances. For his subsequent London seasons, Paderewski raised his fee to two hundred guineas and then to five hundred, a truly exorbitant sum that could be paid only by the select few. See Arthur Hedley, *Chopin*, p. 118 and Paderewski & Lawton, *Memoirs*, p. 181-183

19 "My first tour became a long series of concerts, 107 in all, and before it was over I was asked to return for the following season." From *Memoirs* by Paderewski and Lawton, p. 223

20 From *Paderewski Discovers America* by James H. Phillips, p. 72. The receipts from his second and third American tour reportedly were $160,000 and $248,000, respectively. See Rom Landau: *Paderewski*, p. 75

21 From the *Los Angeles Times*, February 6, 1896. ProQuest Historical Newspapers search. Quoted by permission

~ CHAPTER FOUR ~

AT THE PIANO

Chopin was a rare example of an artist with completely natural musical talent, for whom playing piano was an instinctive act. His innate facility with the instrument obviated the need of spending countless hours on practicing various exercises and learning the basics of piano technique. Chopin's first piano teacher, Wojciech Żywny, was a violinist. As a competent, professional musician he must have had rudimentary piano skills and may have given Chopin some basic guidance on playing the instrument. Otherwise Żywny certainly could not—and did not—teach his pupil how to evoke the startlingly beautiful sonorities and arrive at the complex piano textures that inhabited Chopin's music from the beginning. Instead, Żywny wisely pointed his exceptional student towards the music of Bach, Mozart and some Beethoven, and was content to see Chopin's genius develop and blossom during the six years (1816-1822) he had worked with him.

The same could be said of Chopin's only other teacher, Józef Elsner, with whom Chopin primarily studied music theory and composition. Elsner—one of Poland's most respected composers at that time—took over from Żywny in 1822 as Chopin's private tutor. Four years later, in the fall of 1826, Chopin entered the Warsaw Conservatory and formally continued his studies with Elsner for the next three years. Aside from watching over Chopin's development as a composer (and insisting that Chopin try his hand in such traditional forms as Variations, Sonata, Piano Trio, or Piano Concerto), Elsner largely did not interfere with Chopin's artistic development either. There is only one instance—perhaps in response to a number of early Mazurkas and Polonaises that Chopin wrote at that time—when Elsner apparently advised his pupil against clinging to "one method, one manner, one national idiom as the *non plus ultra* of an artistic model." Quite certain of the road ahead, Chopin responded that he had "the perhaps audacious, but noble, desire to create a new world" for himself.[1]

Always grateful to his music teachers, Chopin took every opportunity to praise both Żywny and Elsner. He did so after his two successful debut concerts in Vienna in 1829, stating that "With Messrs. Elsner and Żywny even the biggest dunderhead would learn."[2] In a letter dated 10 April 1830 and addressed to his friend, Tytus Wojciechowski, Chopin discussed numerous press reviews and notices of his concerts and continued:

You must know that in that article the *Official Bulletin* declared that the Poles should be as proud of me as the Germans are of Mozart; obvious nonsense. […] If I had not been taught by Elsner, who imbued me with convictions, I should doubtless have accomplished still less than I now have.[3]

The warm relationship between the teacher and his student is confirmed in a letter from Chopin to Elsner, dated Paris, 14 December 1831:

Your letter gave me fresh proof of the paternal care and real benevolence which you are still good enough to continue toward the most affectionate of your pupils.

In 1830, though I knew how much I lack and how far I have to go if I am to approach any standard of yours […] I must think of clearing a path for myself in the world as a pianist, putting off till some later time those higher artistic hopes which your letter rightly puts forward. To be a great composer, one must have enormous knowledge, which, as you have taught me, demands not only listening to the work of others, but still more listening to one's own.[4]

Chopin corresponded with Elsner for many years and throughout his life held his teacher's music in high esteem. On several occasions Chopin helped to arrange performances of Elsner's compositions and in 1840 tried to convince his publisher in Paris, Schlesinger, to print Elsner's *Oratorio*.[5]

In the end, Żywny and Elsner merely encouraged Chopin's talent to develop in an organic, self-guided way, and from his late teens Chopin relied solely on his musical instincts to develop his skills as pianist and composer. As a virtuoso performer, Chopin also forged his own path. His phenomenal reputation as a pianist was not based on countless concerts given all across Europe, as was the case with Franz Liszt, for example. After a handful of performances in Poland during the first half of his life, Chopin was heard in Vienna and a few cities in Germany before moving to Paris in 1831. His public appearances there were just as rare: a debut on 26 February 1832, a benefit concert (with Liszt) in April 1833, a Conservatoire appearance in December 1834, two concerts—a charity and a Conservatoire performance—in April 1835, recital at the court and a concert with his friend Alkan in 1838, two chamber music concerts in 1841 and 1842 with cellist Auguste Franchomme (1808-1884) and singer Pauline Viardot (1821-1910), and Chopin's last concert in Paris in February 1848 at Salle Pleyel. After travelling to England, Chopin's public performances included a June 1848 matinee at Madame Sartori's salon concert series at 99 Eaton Place, an early July recital at St. James's Square of Lord Falmouth's House, a "Gentlemen's Concerts" appearance in Manchester in late August, as well as concerts in Glasgow and Edinburgh.

Franz Liszt remembered Chopin's debut concert in Paris and his other public performances during the early 1830s:

He gave several concerts after his arrival in Paris, where he was immediately received and admired in the circles of the elite, as well as welcomed by the young artists. We remember his first appearance in the salons of Pleyel, where the most enthusiastic and redoubled applause seemed scarcely sufficient to express our enchantment for the genius which had revealed new phases of poetic feeling, and made such happy yet bold innovations in the form of musical art.[6]

Figure 17: Chopin in a 1838 portrait by Jakob Götzenberger. Reproduction engraving in the collection of the Jagiellonian University, catalogue no. 475/I. Used by permission

In December of 1834 Chopin played his E minor Piano Concerto at Berlioz's concert at the Paris Conservatoire. Berlioz, whose literary gifts were considerable, described the effect of the Concerto's middle movement on the audience:

The andante transports the auditorium into an ecstatic calm; [...] the last note drops like a pearl in a golden vase, and the audience, absorbed in its contemplation, hold back the applause for a few moments: they are listening still. It is like having watched the half-tints of an evening twilight dissolve harmoniously, and then staying motionless in the darkness, the eyes still fixed on the point in the horizon whence the light has just vanished.[7]

Half a year later, in July of 1835, Chopin travelled to Karlsbad to meet with his family. He later visited Dresden and then continued to Leipzig, where he spent some time with Schumann and Mendelssohn. Schumann's impressions of Chopin performing a few of his Op. 25 Etudes include the following passage:

Imagine an Aeolian harp possessing all the scales, and an artist's hand combining these with all kinds of fantastic embellishments, but always with an audible deep ground bass, and in the treble, a softly flowing cantilena—and you will have some idea of his playing. No wonder, then, that we were most of all charmed with those pieces which we had heard played by himself, and particularly with the first, in A-flat major, rather a poem than an étude. But it would be a mistake to suppose that he allowed us to hear every one of its small notes. It was rather an undulation of the A-flat major chord, brought out more loudly here and there with the pedal. But, exquisitely entangled in the harmony, there ensued a wondrous melody in the big notes. It was only in the middle section that a tenor voice once broke clearly from the chords and joined the principal melody. And when the étude was ended, we felt as though we had seen a lovely picture in a dream, and, half awake, we strove to seize it again; but such things cannot be described, nor can they be fitly praised. Then he played the second in the book, in F minor, again one in which his individuality displays itself in a manner never to be

forgotten; as charming, dreamy and soft as the song of a sleeping child. That in F major followed; fine again, but novel less in its character than in its figuration; here the master shows his admirable powers of that most amiable bravura—but what use are the words?[8]

His rare public appearances aside, Chopin's pianistic reputation largely rests on his salon performances, of which he gave a fair number throughout his life. Everyone who heard him in those intimate gatherings was mesmerized by the beauty of Chopin's music, the spontaneity of his improvisations, and the unprecedented sound effects his hands elicited from the piano. Pianist—and later famous English conductor—Charles Hallé (1819-1895) heard Chopin on 30 November 1836 at a salon in Paris and, in a letter to his parents written only two days later, described his experience as follows:

I went to dine with Baron Eichtal, where I was very cordially treated, and where I heard—*Chopin*. That was beyond all words. The few senses I had have quite left me. I could have jumped into the Seine. Everything I hear now seems so insignificant, that I would rather not hear it at all. Chopin! He is no man, he is an angel, a god (or what can I say more?) Chopin's compositions played by Chopin! That is a joy never to be surpassed.[9]

Hallé returned to this memorable evening in his autobiography, written towards the end of his life:

I heard him play, and was fascinated beyond expression. It seemed to me as if I had got into another world … I sat entranced, filled with wonderment, and if the room had suddenly been peopled with fairies, I should not have been astonished. The marvelous charm, the poetry and originality, the perfect freedom and absolute lucidity of Chopin's playing at that time cannot be described. It was perfection in every sense. He seemed to be pleased with the evident impression he had produced … In listening to him you lost all power of analysis; you did not for a moment think how perfect was his execution of this or that difficulty; you listened, as it were, to the improvisation of a poem, and were under the charm as long as it lasted.[10]

He accomplishes enormous difficulties, but so quietly, so smoothly and with such constant delicacy and refinement that the listener is not sensible of their real magnitude. It is the exquisite delicacy, with the liquid mellowness of his tone, and the pearly roundness of his passages of rapid articulation which are the peculiar features of his execution, while his music is characterized by freedom of thought, varied expression and a kind of romantic melancholy which seems the natural mood of the artist's mind.[11]

———————

Another, quite extensive review of Chopin's matinee in London's West End appeared in the *Daily News* on 10 July 1848. The writer must have been a musician—perhaps also a pianist—who tried to convey the supreme refinement of Chopin's playing:

There was a numerous and fashionable assembly, who were delighted with the entertainment provided for them. M. Chopin performed an *Andante sostenuto* and a Scherzo from his Opus 31, a selection from his celebrated studies, a Nocturne and a *Berceuse* and several of his own Preludes, Mazurkas and Waltzes. In these various pieces he showed very strikingly his original genius as a composer and his transcendental powers as a performer. His music is as strongly marked with individual character as that of any master who has ever lived. It is highly finished, new in its harmonies, full of contrapuntal skill and ingenious contrivance; and yet we have never heard music which has so much the air of unpremeditated effusion. The performer seems to abandon himself to the impulses of his fancy and feeling, to indulge in a reverie and to pour out unconsciously, as it were, the thoughts and emotions that pass through his mind…

A comparison of Chopin's early years at the piano with Paderewski's is quite telling for, when it came to the piano, Paderewski's mastery of the instrument came only after a long and torturous process that included numerous teachers and countless hours of laborious practicing. Whatever talent for the instrument Paderewski possessed, it had little chance to blossom during his youth under a few highly inadequate instructors and rather primitive conditions existing in the provincial towns of Podolia in the middle of the nineteenth century. Living far away from any cultural center, Paderewski had almost no experience of concert life and of the artistic environment that Chopin enjoyed in Poland's capital during the first two decades of his life. Even when Paderewski arrived with his father in Warsaw at the age of twelve and was admitted to the Music Institute[12] without examination, his dream of becoming a pianist seemed far from certain:

Although I was only twelve years old, and up to that time had had no real piano instruction, I already realized, or perhaps I should say sensed, what kind of a teacher I needed. So I went to my first lesson at the Conservatory with an eagerness that would be impossible for me to describe. I feel that emotion still—to this day. It had never occurred to me that I should meet disappointment there, that I should again be defeated in my anxiety to learn how to play. My childish idea was that the Conservatory would solve all my problems—that I should fall into the right hands at once. But the first teacher I saw was so discouraging and so unpleasant, that I asked at once to be relieved from piano study. He said I had not the hands for piano playing, and many other things as well. […] The second piano teacher I went to was a very emotional man … and he admitted and realized at once that I really had something to say with my fingers. "Oh yes," he said, "you are talented. There is no doubt about that. You have a real and natural gift." But his own piano playing must have been in his youth very much like mine, because he did not pay the necessary attention to the technical difficulties. I came across such teachers all the time. Such cruelty of Fate![13]

As a result, in Warsaw Paderewski began to study music theory and composition, and tried to learn playing several different wind instruments, including the flute, oboe, clarinet, bassoon, French horn, and the trombone. Dissatisfied with being forced to study everything but the piano, Paderewski left the Music Institute and tried to organize a summer concert tour of eastern Poland for himself and two of his friends. When this proved spectacularly unsuccessful, Paderewski reluctantly returned to complete his studies in Warsaw. When he finally graduated and performed Grieg's Piano Concerto with an orchestra, he did not feel he accomplished much; the family situation notwithstanding, he decided to continue studying, this time in Berlin. Here again, Paderewski mainly studied composition and occasionally returned to Poland to perform as a pianist. It was not until he was twenty-four that Paderewski finally came to Vienna and asked the famous pianist and esteemed pedagogue, Teodor Leschetizky, to become his teacher. Leschetizky at first was quite puzzled why an adult who already performed in public should come to him with the hope of becoming a concert pianist:

"And you intend to make a repertoire, to start study now as a virtuoso, at your age? Do you realize what you are saying? It's impossible, I tell you." […] My world crumbled into ruins in those few moments. Finally he stopped his walk, pulled himself together and said, "Well, at any rate play me something—play something for me now, it does not matter what." So I played; of course, my compositions. He listened very attentively—quietly—then he said, "You have a great many qualities as a pianist. You have a *natural* technique, but it lacks so very much. But still you have the principal *quality*, that is *tone*. Without having studied, you already know how to vary that tone, how to give different expressions with your fingers alone, and there is still something else which is quite remarkable, and that is—your pedaling! That is perhaps the most extraordinary thing, that any one who has not seriously studied the piano can realize the enormous importance of pedaling. But you are a musician, I see, and it is that musical instinct that leads you in using so properly the principal means of expression—the pedal. But, I am afraid there will be too much to do with your fingers, because they lack *absolutely discipline!* […] I'm afraid you do not know *how to work!*" He put his finger on it immediately. My tragedy! My heart almost lost a beat at these fateful worlds. I was fearful that he would not accept me as a pupil. "If I decide to give you a few lessons," he continued, "you must start with *finger exercises* and some Czerny studies." A pupil again![14]

Four years later, by dint of extraordinary discipline, unceasing hard work and total concentration, Paderewski succeeded against all odds in achieving his goal. At the time of his debut in Paris he was already twenty-eight, hardly the propitious age for any artist to enter the concert stage. Fortunately, Paderewski's charismatic performance, highly polished technique developed under the watchful eye of Leschetizky, full and noble tone, and refined use of pedal that produced a wide spectrum of sonorities, made for a triumphant launch of his career. Paderewski's youthful appearance and the mass of auburn hair were also a factor in the fascination of the public with this young Polish virtuoso. Although Paderewski's 1888 Paris debut was a watershed moment, he realized more than anyone else in his audience that the work of being a concert pianist was just beginning. He had to learn new repertoire, and this onerous task took endless hours of practicing before and during his tours. When Paderewski arrived in New York in November 1891, he found the schedule of his appearances totally overwhelming:

I had imagined that [the tour] would be graduated, at first starting with a few concerts, then a little rest, then more concerts, etc. But no, nothing of the sort, it was concert after concert with only a day or two between: a continuous tour, and I had to begin in New York with *three orchestral* concerts, at which I had to play *six* piano concertos in one week and a group of solos. […] It was six concertos or nothing! True, I had four of them ready, but the other two, although I played them once or twice, were not in my opinion yet ready for public performance. Why, in Europe I might not have an opportunity of playing six concertos in one season. […] But in New York, I was expected to play six concertos in one week! I was completely dazed at first. The dreadful knowledge of what faced me had a paralyzing effect. At that moment I longed for the earth to open and swallow me up. It was superhuman. Perhaps now, after all these years, I should be able to accommodate such a colossal thing after a long preparation, but then, at the beginning of my career, with my small experience and at such short notice, it was something really terrific. […] But somehow, I gathered my courage together and started practicing. I must add that after the week of six concertos (already advertised) I had in addition to play six recitals. These recitals were scheduled for the following two weeks, which meant practically a concert every other day and a different program each time. […][15]

In order to fulfill the terms of his contract, Paderewski spent the nights after each of his New York concert practicing his programs for the recital on the following day. One of these practice sessions lasted seventeen hours and, as Paderewski later admitted in his *Memoirs*, "My arms were dropping off."[16] Such utter physical exhaustion was Paderewski's constant companion because he habitually worked very long hours throughout his career in order to prepare his programs. Paderewski always travelled across the United States on a luxuriously-appointed Pullman rail car equipped with a piano, library, self-contained heating system and a private telephone line that was always connected to the local phone exchange wherever he stopped to perform. He practiced at every opportunity when his train was not moving; otherwise during his journeys he chatted with a variety of guests and crew on board. Paderewski's permanent entourage included his personal secretary, a Creole chef and an assistant cook, a valet, two Pullman porters and a few representatives of the Steinway Company.[17]

Paderewski's long friendship with the Steinway family and Steinway pianos dated from his first American tour, which was organized by them. As magnificent and full-sounding as Steinway pianos were, they required significantly more strength to play them since their keyboard mechanism was much heavier than European pianos on which Paderewski had heretofore performed. Since he could not constantly perform on such heavy-action instruments, Paderewski eventually persuaded Steinway technicians to regulate the pianos he used in concerts to his liking. Unfortunately during his recital in Rochester, New York, Paderewski encountered a very heavy Steinway and, after playing a program and suffering terrible pain, he realized that he had seriously injured his arm. From that point on, Paderewski's concerts in America depended on occasional visits to doctors, who applied a variety of remedies for his ailing hands. During his second American tour in 1893, Paderewski's arms and fingers were still far from healed and, as soon as he returned to Europe, he was forced to take a longer break from the concert stage and turn his attention to composing instead.

Keen to refine his technique and expand his repertoire, Paderewski also continued to practice extensively at home. This was one of his ways of securing a well-controlled performance.

Figure 18: Paderewski in the early 1900s. Polish Music Center Archives, the Zygmunt and Luisa Stojowski Collection. All rights reserved

In fact, throughout his life Paderewski suffered from stage fright and insisted on very specific conditions in the concert halls where he appeared. His specially-designed piano chair had to be positioned in a very precise way (his personal Steinway technician saw to this every time), the concert hall lights had to be dimmed, and the auditorium had to be amply heated.

Paderewski hated drafts and bathed his hands in hot water before going out on stage. All these precautions did not make performing easier—being an absolute perfectionist, Paderewski constantly worried about possible defects in his playing. The young Polish pianist, Artur Rubinstein (1887-1982) visited Paderewski's Swiss residence in 1902 and remembered that Paderewski was "repeating certain difficult passages slowly a hundred times."[18]

Having reached middle age, Paderewski's never-ending chain of traveling and performing inevitably led to a serious health crisis. During his ninth American tour, which began in October 1913, Paderewski experienced not only a great deal of physical fatigue but also suffered from a case of severe pain in his right arm. Canceling all concert engagements, Paderewski and his wife, Helena, hastily set out for San Francisco:

I had a severe attack of neuritis in my right arm. It was so painful that I played with extreme difficulty, and I felt that the moment soon would come when I should have to interrupt my tour. Well, that moment came in Seattle. I could not play any longer. I could not even lift my arm, the pain was intolerable, and as I was to proceed from Seattle through Portland, Oregon, to San Francisco, I cancelled the concert in Seattle and went directly to San Francisco. This condition was not only aggravated but actually brought about by the terrific nervous strain and anxiety of the past months. […]

I was very anxiously awaiting the arrival of [a] doctor when Mr. Urchs returned, not with the doctor but with another friend of mine, a musician from San Francisco, Sir Henry Heymann, and he said, "Now, there is no use calling a doctor, because a doctor cannot cure you immediately and that's what you want. But there is something else for you to do. You must go at once to Paso Robles and take some of the mud baths there for your arm. They are magical," Heymann said, "so many of my friends have been cured, and I am also enjoying the treatment myself because I too have neuritis badly. It is almost infallible, that treatment at Paso Robles."

It was only six hours away from San Francisco and worth trying. So we started immediately for Paso Robles, and there I had my treatment for three weeks, after which I could continue my tour and finish it in comfort. My neuritis had left me. That place is absolutely unknown, and, as I know by my own experience, the result of that treatment is really miraculous.[19]

Thus began yet another of Paderewski's adventures. Having initially come to the Central California town of Paso Robles in January of 1914 for a cure, after recovering Paderewski decided to invest in local real estate. True to form, Paderewski's land investments—like everything else he did—were on a truly epic scale. Within a few weeks spent in Paso Robles, Paderewski bought about 3000 acres of ranchland that he eventually turned into almond groves and vineyards. In fact, Paderewski became one of the most important early growers of Zinfandel and Syrah grapes in California. He also invested in oil exploration by purchasing over 2600 acres

of land south of Paso Robles on the outskirts of the town of Santa Maria.

In the meantime, World War I broke out in Europe and Paderewski resolved to put his

Figure 19: Paderewski his almond grove, Paso Robles, 1921. The Paso Robles Collection, Polish Music Center, USC.

pianistic career on hold and lend his considerable talents and political connections to the cause of fighting for Poland's independence. He was instrumental in convincing President Wilson to include a clause stipulating the political and geographical framework for independent Poland after the war. As this seemingly inconceivable goal became realized, Paderewski became the first Prime Minister of independent Poland in 1919. After playing a historical role in securing a democratic government for his homeland, he served as its delegate to the League of Nations.

With Poland's independence seemingly secure, by 1922 Paderewski decided to leave politics and return to the concert stage. It was an unprecedented move for a musician who was then approaching retirement age. Against all odds, Paderewski succeeded in a spectacular fashion and his 1922 comeback as a concert pianist was a phenomenal and unqualified success. The musical elite and countless friends and fans rose to their feet as Paderewski appeared on stage of Carnegie Hall in New York, paying tribute to an extraordinary artist and a man of epic historical achievements. Press reports and reviews were uniformly superlative, many noting that Paderewski's artistry had now reached even more sublime heights. The words of Ernest Newman, the preeminent English critic, perfectly sum up the public reaction to Paderewski's second coming: "There is no other living pianist who can reveal so acute a sensibility to the poetic content of music." From that point on Paderewski triumphantly toured the world, playing concerts and visiting with royalty, presidents, prime ministers, and other heads of state. He also generously performed for numerous charitable causes, accepted honors from several universities, and became a superstar for audiences of millions.

Always magnanimous to those in need, throughout his life Paderewski generously contributed to all kinds of charitable causes. Perhaps the most spectacular of these benefits was Paderewski's 1932 performance at Madison Square Garden. Artistically, it was one of his greatest triumphs; critics and the audience sixteen thousand went wild with applause. The concert concluded Paderewski's 1932 tour of the United States and raised $37,000 for unemployed American musicians.

Although Paderewski did not like to record and hated radio broadcasts, he was nonetheless persuaded to appear in a 1937 film, *Moonlight*

Figure 20: A still from Paderewski's film, *Moonlight Sonata* (1937). The Paso Robles Collection, Polish Music Center, USC.

Sonata, directed by Lothar Mendes. In it, Paderewski gives a breathtaking recital of works by Beethoven, Liszt, Chopin, and also plays his own *Menuet*. This remarkable film gives priceless insights into Paderewski's admirable piano technique and his magisterial interpretations of the repertoire classics. The viewer also sees a good dose of Paderewski, who amply demonstrates his natural gift for acting. His stage talent was spotted early on by Paderewski's teacher, Leschetizky, who—according to Charles Phillips—had said, "He could have been successful either as a diplomat or as an actor if he had chosen."[20]

During the course of his long life, Paderewski made twenty tours of the United States. His last took place in 1939 when he was seventy-nine and already a living legend for the generations of audiences from all over the world. Paderewski appeared on the cover of *Time Magazine* twice (in 1928 and 1939) and throughout the 1920s and the 1930s he played to sold-out halls. His last recital in Los Angeles on 2 April 1939 is a good example of the incredible loyalty of his public. Tickets for the concert were sold out in one hour and the enormous Shrine Auditorium was filled to capacity. The *Los Angeles Times* headline caught the spirit of that remarkable evening: "Paderewski's Courage and Artistry Capture City—Eight thousand Enthralled at Concert of Polish Musician and Statesman." Paderewski's 1939 tour ended in May when he became indisposed just before his recital at the Madison Square Garden in New York City and his appearance had to be cancelled at the very last minute. As it turned out, Paderewski would never perform again.

When it came to concert programs and performing repertoire, Chopin's and Paderewski's stage appearances differed greatly. This was mainly due to the fact that Chopin lived in the age of the composer-virtuoso, who basically performed exclusively his own works. Such, after all, was the established tradition: Bach, Haydn, Mozart, and Beethoven are the most obvious examples of artists who almost exclusively presented their own music to their audiences. With the rise of public concerts during the nineteenth century, a new type of musician appeared on stage—a performer-interpreter of works by other composers, who was not necessarily a composer himself. As a composer and virtuoso, Franz Liszt straddled these two worlds by championing the formula of a public recital, where he performed Beethoven's Sonatas and works by other composers in addition to showcasing his music. Mendelssohn— another great pianist, composer and conductor— contributed greatly to the revival of Bach's music by bringing back to concert halls the forgotten masterpieces from the Baroque era. Robert Schumann who wanted to become a virtuoso but injured his hand in the process of excessive practicing, became a composer; his wife, Clara, an acclaimed virtuoso in her own right, premiered not only all of Schumann's music, but also programmed Beethoven, Chopin, and Brahms, among others, in her concerts.

Paderewski, on the other hand, lived on the cusp of the modern age of performers who are mainly interpreters of the instrumental repertoire and only rarely compose their own music. Nonetheless, in spite of his career being devoted to programming music by many different composers, Paderewski often placed some of his music on his solo recitals and appearances with orchestras. Thus, the kinds of repertoire Chopin and Paderewski presented in concert during their lives differed significantly in many respects.

While Chopin mostly performed his own compositions, he occasionally played music by other composers as well. Johann Sebastian Bach was certainly one of Chopin's favorites and his cycle of forty-eight Preludes and Fugues constituted part of Chopin's piano practicing routine. When one of his students asked him how he prepares for concerts, Chopin replied:

For a fortnight I shut myself up and play Bach. That's my preparation. I don't practice my own compositions.[21]

Chopin was introduced to Bach's music early on by his teachers in Warsaw. He considered Bach's highly complex polyphonic music necessary for pianistic education (*l'indispensable du pianiste*)[22] and kept Bach's Preludes and Fugues in his repertoire throughout his life. Occasionally he performed them during lessons, as related by one of his students, Friederike Streicher (1816-1895):

> One morning he played from memory fourteen Preludes and Fugues of Bach's, and when I expressed my joyful admiration at this unparalleled performance, he replied: "Cela ne s'oublie jamais."[23]

There is also one instance of Chopin performing Bach's Concerto for Three Keyboards at a December 1833 concert in Paris with his friends Franz Liszt and Ferdinand Hiller. Evidently, Chopin also recommended Bach's Keyboard Suites to his students. Besides Bach, Wolfgang Amadeus Mozart was the other composer whose music Chopin clearly held in the highest esteem. Chopin's highly refined piano touch with its infinite variety of shading was ideally suited to Mozart's music and he programmed Mozart's chamber works on several occasions, most notably for his last performance at Salle Pleyel in February of 1848. Chopin also had several of Beethoven's Piano Sonatas in his repertoire and played at least one of them, Op. 26, for his students, as well as one of Beethoven's Piano Concertos.[24] Chopin's repertoire also included music by his contemporaries: Muzio Clementi, John Field, Johann Nepomuk Hummel, Carl Maria von Weber, Felix Mendelssohn, and Ignaz Moscheles, whose *Grande Sonate*, Op. 47, for piano four hands, Chopin performed with Liszt and Moscheles on a few occasions.[25]

Chopin's student, Karol Mikuli (1821-1897) described the scope of his teacher's repertoire as follows:

> Although Chopin played mostly his own compositions, he had all the great and beautiful works of the piano literature in his memory—a memory as highly developed as it was reliable. Above all he prized Bach, and between Bach and Mozart it is hard to say whom he loved more. His interpretation of their music was of unrivalled greatness […] Naturally, Beethoven was also close to his heart. Chopin took particular pleasure in playing the work of Weber, particularly the *Concertstück* and the Sonatas in A-flat major and E minor; Hummel's Fantasy, Septet and concertos; Field's Concerto in A-flat major and his Nocturnes, to which he would improvise the most beautiful *Fioritures*.[26]

An anonymous Scottish lady, who studied with Chopin in Paris in the mid 1840s, remembered the impromptu performance of Beethoven's Op. 26 Sonata:

[Chopin] took my place and played the entire Sonata. It was like a revelation [...] He played that *Marche funèbre* of Beethoven's with a grand, orchestral, powerfully dramatic effect, yet with a sort of restrained emotion which was indescribable. Lastly he rushed throughout the final movement with faultless precision and extraordinary delicacy—not a single note lost, and with marvelous phrasing and alternation of light and shade. We stood spellbound, never having heard the like.[27]

Georges Mathias (1826-1910) studied with Chopin for about six years and later in his long life became a professor of piano at the Paris Conservatoire. During his thirty years of teaching he worked with many talented pianists and passed on Chopin's performing tradition to several future generations of musicians. A child prodigy, Mathias began studying with Chopin around 1839, when he was thirteen. He vividly remembered Chopin's playing:

First of all, those who have heard Chopin may well say that nothing remotely resembling his playing has ever been heard since. His playing was like his music; and what virtuosity! What power! Yes, what power! Though it would only last for a few bars; and the exaltation, the inspiration! The whole man vibrated! The piano became so intensely animated that it gave one shivers. I repeat that the instrument which one heard Chopin playing never existed except beneath Chopin's fingers: he played as he composed... Chopin, performer of genius, interpreted Mozart, Beethoven with the feeling of Chopin, and it was extremely beautiful, it was sublime.[28]

Emile Gaillard (1821-1902) was a banker and amateur pianist, who studied with Chopin. One of Chopin's late Mazurkas (without the opus number) is dedicated to him. He too recalled Chopin's extraordinary performances, filled with delicacy and refinement, unlike many of the Romantic-era virtuosos who occasionally destroyed pianos by pounding heavily on them:

Chopin never flattened his piano, and yet, under his fingers, everything came out wonderfully. While his left hand played a beautiful song, straight from the heart, his right hand would seem casually to unfold a magnificent lacework of sound. Virtuosity disappeared behind the emotion; one was less dazzled than moved. He appeared to caress the keyboard, while his sensitive and grieving soul rose and wandered freely among us. When he finished playing a Nocturne one wished only to be quiet so that the enchantment should not be broken. He himself, on finishing a piece, would often remain sitting at the keyboard in silence, pursuing a dream of his own.[29]

Chopin's performances of his own music left his listeners hypnotized by the incredibly poetic atmosphere combined with the absolute and unobtrusive mastery of piano technique. Mendelssohn, a brilliant pianist himself, had an opportunity to spend some time at the piano with Chopin and Ferdinand Hiller (1811-1885), as both were visiting the Rhenish Music Festival in Germany. They stopped in Aachen and continued on to Düsseldorf, where they made music together with Mendelssohn, who reported to his mother on 23 May 1834:

> […] The three of us were at the piano, which afforded me great pleasure. […] As a pianist Chopin is now one of the greatest of all—doing things as original as Paganini does on the violin, and bringing about miracles that one would never have believed possible.[30]

Hiller, who was Chopin's close friend in Paris in the 1830s and often performed with him in concert, wrote:

> […] I must describe his wonderful playing, which will remain impressed on my soul until I draw my last breath. I have said that he rarely opened his heart out; but at the piano he abandoned himself more completely than any other musician I have ever heard—with such concentration that all extraneous thoughts simply fell away. Nobody before had stirred the keys of a grand piano like that, nor known how to release such countless sonorities from it. Rhythmic firmness was combined with freedom in the declamation of his melodies, so that they would seem to have occurred to him at that very moment. What in the hands of others was elegant embellishment, in his hands became a colorful wreath of flowers; what in others was technical dexterity seemed in his playing like the flight of a swallow. All thought of isolating any one quality—novelty, grace, perfection, soul—fell away; it was simply Chopin. […] Even the deepest understanding of his compositions and the most intimate familiarity with them can give no idea of the poetry of address that was his very own. All material considerations vanished—it was like the light of a wonderful meteor, bewitching us all the more with its unfathomable mystery.[31]

La France musicale published a review of Chopin's 21 February 1842 concert at Salle Pleyel, given with singer Pauline Viardot and cellist Auguste Franchomme. According to the concert program Chopin performed several of his solo piano compositions: *Andante suivi de la 3e Ballade; Suite de Nocturne, Préludes et Etudes; Nocturne, Préludes, Mazurkas et Impromptu.* The magazine correspondent conveyed the atmosphere of this brilliant evening by concentrating on the beauty of Chopin's compositions and the sounds he elicited from the instrument:

Figure 21: A commemorative medal with Ferdinand Hiller and Frederic Chopin from 1848. Polish Music Center Archives, USC

A poet, and a tender poet above all, Chopin makes poetry predominate. He creates prodigious difficulties of performance, but never to the detriment of his melody, which is always simple and original. Follow the pianist's hands and see the marvelous ease with which he performs the most graceful runs, draws together the width of the keyboard, passes successively from *piano* to *forte* and from *forte* to *piano*! M. Pleyel's magnificent instruments lend themselves admirably to these various shadings. Listening to all these sounds, all these nuances—which follow each other, intermingle, separate and reunite to arrive at the same goal, melody—one might well believe one is hearing small fairy voices sighing under silver bells, or a rain of pearls falling on crystal tables. The pianist's fingers seem to multiply ad inifinitum; it does not appear possible that only two hands can produce effects of rapidity so precisely and naturally. Do not ask Chopin to simulate grand orchestral effects on the piano. This type of playing suits neither his constitution nor his ideas. […] His inspiration is all of tender and naïve poetry; do not ask him for big gestures or diabolic variations; he wishes to speak to the heart, not to the eyes; he wishes to love you, not to devour you. See: the public is in ecstasy; enthusiasm is at its peak: Chopin has achieved his aim.[32]

Paderewski's concert programs were vast and often stretched to well over two hours of very intense music making. In addition to the repertoire listed in the program, numerous encores were demanded by his audiences at the end. Paderewski's afternoon recitals that began between three and four o'clock were often wrapping up around seven in the evening.[33] In his performances Paderewski drew on a very large repertoire of solo music that represented almost the entire spectrum of piano literature.[34] Unlike Chopin, Paderewski played relatively little of Bach's music, with the *Chromatic Fantasy and Fugue* being the only piece that he regularly programmed in concert; he also featured Liszt's transcriptions of Bach's works. Besides Bach, a few short pieces by Domenico Scarlatti and George Friedrich Handel rounded off Paderewski's repertoire of Baroque era music.

Chopin's other great favorite—Mozart—was represented on Paderewski's concerts only by the A major Sonata KV 331 and the A minor Rondo. Of other composers from the Classical period, Paderewski programmed Haydn's F minor Variations which, especially during his tours of the United States in the late 1920s and the 1930, were used as an opening piece for many of his recitals.

Beethoven's music, however, always had a prominent place on Paderewski's programs. He was very fond of Beethoven's Sonatas, and throughout his life he played most of them, especially favoring the two great middle period Sonatas (the *Waldstein* and the *Appassionata*) as well as the magnificent last four Sonatas, Op. 101, 109, 110, and 111. He also often performed Beethoven's 32 Variations in C minor, especially on his earlier tours, and occasionally performed the E-flat Piano Concerto, Op. 73 with orchestras.

Music by Franz Schubert and Robert Schumann often figured on Paderewski's concerts throughout his life and he was acknowledged as an excellent interpreter of German Romantic music. Schubert's Impromptus and *Moments Musicaux* as well as Schumann's Piano Sonatas in F-sharp minor and G minor, *Carnaval*, *Fantasia in C major*, *Etudes Symphoniques*, *Fantasiestücke*, *Nachtstücke*, *Waldszenen*, and the famous *Toccata* regularly found their way to his programs. On occasion, Paderewski also performed selected *Songs without Words* and *Variations Sérieuses* by Mendelssohn, and the demanding *Paganini Variations* by Brahms. Shorter items by other Romantic composers—Enrique Granados, Maurycy Moszkowski, Zygmunt Noskowski, Anton Rubinstein, Camille Saint-Saëns, Alexander Scriabin, Zygmunt Stojowski, and Aleksander Zarzycki—often served as encores after the main program. The public also demanded (and usually received) an encore of Paderewski's own celebrated *Menuet*, *Cracovienne fantastique*, or one of many of his charming salon pieces written in the 1880s.

From among the contemporary composers, Paderewski played only a few pieces by Claude Debussy, Gabriel Fauré, Ernest Schelling, Giovanni Sgambati, and his younger colleague and fellow Pole, Karol Szymanowski.

Paderewski was quite fond of chamber music and played a good deal of it, especially in the early years of his career. Already during his studies in Warsaw, he formed a trio with two friends from the Musical Institute and toured with them a little. After graduating he gave concerts in Warsaw, Kraków, Zakopane, Berlin, and Paris with the violinist Władysław Górski, who was an older friend from Warsaw and whose household for a time became Paderewski's second home. Paderewski also briefly lived with the Adamowski family in Warsaw; their son Tymoteusz was a violinist, and the other son, Józef, a cellist. The Adamowski brothers later resettled in America and became members of the Boston Symphony Orchestra. When Paderewski's tour of America took him to Boston, he renewed his friendship with the two brothers and, in the following years, he performed in concert with the Adamowski Quartet. Another opportunity for chamber music arose during Paderewski's one year appointment as professor of piano in Strasbourg in 1885. Besides teaching,

Paderewski played many chamber music concerts throughout the region with his Conservatory faculty colleagues and local musicians. His chamber music repertoire included Beethoven's famous Archduke Trio, the Piano Quartet and Piano Quintet of Brahms, Rubinstein's Trio in B major, Schumann's Piano Quartet and Piano Quintet, as well as a number of violin and piano sonatas.

Undoubtedly the pride of place in Paderewski's recitals was always reserved for Chopin's music. His intuitive interpretations of Chopin's music was noticed by the prominent Polish composer, Władysław Żeleński, even before Paderewski became a household name around the world. Writing in 1883 for the magazine *Czas* [Time], Żeleński observed that:

> Mr. Paderewski charmed everyone with a most beautiful performance of Chopin's Ballade in A-flat major. The calm of the opening and the subsequent gradation of the dynamic force were handled with excellence. Clear phrasing highlighted all of the pathos intended by the composer. As a pianist, Mr. Paderewski has a bright future, and as a composer—perhaps—even brighter one… A Polish soul is sensed throughout. Mr. Paderewski's talent augurs well for the future of Polish music… May God grant him the ability to continue on this path, and we shall welcome in Mr. Paderewski an artist whose name will bring pride to Polish art…[35]

From that point on, in countless recitals all over the world, Paderewski was seen as the torch-bearer of Poland's heroic pianistic tradition. Placed on such a pedestal and bathed in the light of immortality during his lifetime, Paderewski became a favorite subject for poets. In his *Portrait of a Lady*, T.S. Elliot wrote:

> We have been, let us say, to hear the latest Pole
> Transmit the Preludes, through his hair and fingertips.
> "So intimate, this Chopin, that I think his soul
> Should be resurrected only among friends
> Some two or three, who will not touch the bloom
> That is rubbed and questioned in the concert room."

Paderewski indeed "transmitted" to his audiences most of Chopin's compositions that included both Piano Concertos, the Four Ballades, Four Scherzos, the B-flat minor and the B minor Sonatas, Preludes, most of the Polonaises, Nocturnes, Waltzes, Etudes and Mazurkas. Of Paderewski's interpretations of Chopin, the American music critic, writer and pianist Lawrence Gilman wrote:

> And who can play Chopin with Paderewski's flame-edged grace, his blend of fire and tenderness, his superb distinction of style? Who else can discourse to us with those strange accessions of divine madness that seize upon this uncompanioned artist? […] It may be Chopin's exquisite and familiar Butterfly Etude […] Perhaps it is a Chopin Scherzo, romantic, reckless, full of wild agitated runs streaming over the sweetness of wistful chordings; or the pure cradle-song tenderness of the *Berceuse* with its double chromatic runs, its far-off sound of a sunken bell.[36]

The American music critic, James Huneker, wrote an extensive review of Paderewski's 1891 New York debut in the *Musical Courier*. Besides being a writer and author of numerous books on a great variety of subjects, Huneker had a very impressive background as a pianist after studying in Paris with Chopin's student, Georges Mathias, and with Rafael Joseffy, a student of Liszt, in America.

Ignace Jan Paderewski played the piano last night at the new Music Hall, and played it in such a wonderful manner as to see a huge audience mad with enthusiasm and recall memories of Rubinstein in his prime, but a Rubinstein technically infallible. In the dual role of a composer and virtuoso Mr. Paderewski won a triumph that was genuine and nobly deserved, for he is a new personality in music that will bear curious and close study. As to the physical side of his art, he is one of those virtuosi to whom the keyboard has no hidden secrets. His technical equipment is perfect and is used in such an exquisitely musical fashion that the virtuoso merges ever into the artist and mere brutal display and brilliant charlatanry are totally absent. […]

In the group of soli by his fellow countryman, Frédéric Chopin, Paderewski revealed himself as an interpreter who ranks as high as any Chopin player we have yet heard in the city. He has the true subtle poetic capricious spirit, the "żal" to use the Polish word, and his tender sadness and majestic sorrow in the great C minor Nocturne were admirably expressed. He played the A-flat Prélude, with its imploring cadences, and followed with the familiar C-sharp minor Valse, but not rendered familiarly by him. In point of finesse he vied with that arch master of finesse, de Pachmann, and in the C major Etude (Op. 10, no. 7) his lightness of wrist caused the double note figure to actually shimmer on the keyboard. That this self-same Etude, which serves a technical purpose, was delivered so poetically proves Paderewski's innate musical nature.

He sang the lullaby of the F major Ballade, so seldom played, charmingly, and thundered out its climaxes until the noble Steinway grand upon which he played sounded like a veritable orchestra. By the manner of his playing the A-flat Polonaise, which is topsy-turvied by most pianists in order to show how fast they can play, Paderewski administered a gentle reproof, for he took it a true polonaise tempo, a stately, dignified dance, and right chivalric he made its measures. His octave crescendo in the middle part was marvelous in its gradation of tone and elasticity of wrists. In fact his wrist work, notably in double octave trills, is herculean in its power and intensity. […]

Paderewski is a great pianist, one the greatest who has yet visited our shores, and his marked musical abilities as a composer, his superb skill as a virtuoso, when taken in conjunction with his age, concur in making him a youth favored by the gods.[37]

In his 1911 book, *Franz Liszt*, the same James Huneker summarized the phenomenon of Paderewski's astonishing pianism and his enduring popularity:

His tone was noble, his technic adequate, his single-finger touch singing. Above all, there was a romantic temperament exposed; not morbid but robust. His strange appearance, the golden aureoled head, the shy attitude, were rather puzzling to public and critic at his début. Not too much enthusiasm was exhibited during the concert or next morning in the newspapers. But the second performance settled the question. A great artist was revealed. His diffidence melted in the heat of frantic applause. He played the Schumann Concerto, the F minor Concerto of Chopin, many other concertos, all of Chopin's music, much of Schumann, Beethoven, and Liszt. His recitals, first given in the concert hall of Madison Square Garden, so expanded in attendance that he moved to Carnegie Hall. There, with only his piano, Paderewski repeated the Liszt miracle. And year after year. Never in America has a public proved so insatiable in its desire to hear a virtuoso. It is the same from New Orleans to Seattle. Everywhere crowded halls, immense enthusiasms. Now to set all this down to an exotic personality, to occult magnetism, to sensationalism, would be unfair to Paderewski and to the critical discrimination of his audiences. Many have gone to gaze upon him, but they remained to listen. His solid attainments as a musician, his clear, elevated style, his voluptuous, caressing touch, his sometimes exaggerated sentiment, his brilliancy, endurance, and dreamy poetry— these qualities are real, not imaginary. [...]

He is intellectual and his readings of the classics are sane. Of poetic temperament, he is at his best in Chopin, not Beethoven. Eclectic is the best word to apply to his interpretations. He plays programmes from Bach to Liszt with commendable fidelity and versatility. He has the power of rousing his audience from a state of calm indifference to wildest frenzy. [...] I assure you I have been at Paderewski's recitals where my judgments were in abeyance, where my individuality was merged in that of the mob, where I sat and wondered if I really heard; or was Paderewski only going through the motions and not actually touching the keys? His is a static as well as a dramatic art. The tone wells up from the instrument, is not struck. It floats languorously in the air, it seems to pause, transfixed in the air. The Sarmatian melancholy of Paderewski, his deep sensibility, his noble nature, are translated into the music. [...]

In certain things of Chopin he is unapproachable. He plays the F minor Concerto and the E-flat minor Scherzo—from the Second Sonata—beautifully, and if he is not so convincing in the Beethoven Sonata, his interpretation of the E-flat Emperor Concerto is surprisingly free from *morbidezza*; it is direct, manly, and musical. [...] He is more interesting than most pianists because he is more musical; he has more personal charm; there is the feeling when you hear him that he is a complete man, a harmonious artist, and this feeling is very compelling.[38]

Paderewski's recitals invariably ended on a bravura piece by Liszt, including the *Don Juan Fantasy*, a choice from among the *Hungarian Rhapsodies* or Concert Etudes, or concert transcriptions and paraphrases of works by Mendelssohn, Schubert or Paganini. Towards the end of his life, Paderewski liked to close his programs with Liszt's masterly transcription of *Isolde's Love-Death* from Wagner's opera, *Tristan und Isolde*.

Looking at Paderewski's stellar career from a long-studied perspective, Paderewski's favorite biographer, Charles Phillips wrote in 1934:

When Paderewski plays he speaks the language of Heaven. To hear him is a spiritual experience. That is the secret of his effect on his audiences. And the secret of his life's success, of his world-wide influence for good, is simply this: He has a spiritual background. No man rises higher than his source. Paderewski draws off from a high and spiritual source. Therefore he rises high. And he lifts others up.[39]

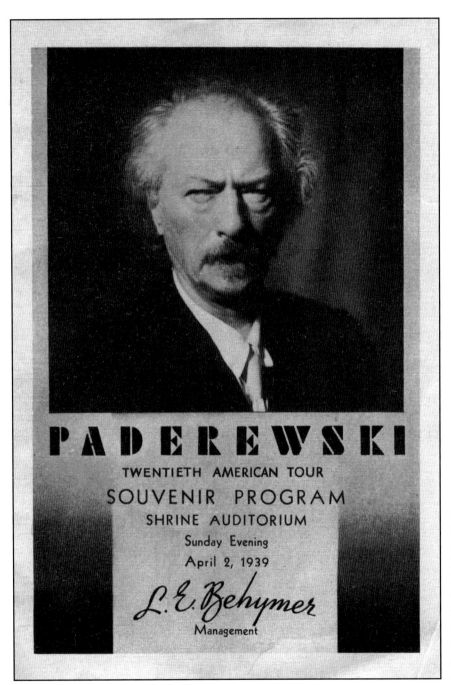

Figure 22: Cover of Paderewski's last recital in Los Angeles. His program on that occasion included Haydn's F minor Variations; Mozart's A minor Rondo; Beethoven's Sonata Op. 57; Chopin's Ballade in F minor, Nocturne in B major, and Mazurka in F-sharp minor, Op. 59; Schubert's *Impromptu*, and Liszt's transcription of Wagner's *Isolde's Love-Death*. Polish Music Center Archives, USC.

1   See Arthur Hedley, *Chopin*, p. 152
2   Ibid., p. 34
3   See *Chopin's Letters*, p. 81
4   Ibid., p. 159-160
5   See Chopin's letter from Paris, dated 24 July 1840
6   See Franz Liszt, *Life of Chopin*, p. 110
7   See Eigeldinger, *Chopin: Pianist and Teacher*, p. 67
8   See Robert Schumann, *On Music and Musicians*, p. 136-137
9   See Eigeldinger, *Chopin: Pianist and Teacher*, p. 271
10 Ibid., p. 271
11 See Arthur Hedley, *Chopin*, p. 120-121
12 Although Paderewski referred to the school he attended in Warsaw as the "Conservatory" its proper name was the Warsaw Music Institute.
13 See Paderewski & Lawton, *Memoirs*, p. 36
14 Ibid., p. 86-87
15 Ibid., p. 193
16 Ibid., p. 197
17 Paderewski's wife, Baroness Helena Rosen, joined him on tours after they were married in 1899. This made for an even larger entourage, since Madame Paderewska came on board with her secretary and a maid. In the concert program for Paderewski's last concert in Los Angeles (2 April 1939), there are several interesting vignettes of Paderewski's travel routines. One of them, entitled "How Paderewski Lives When on Tour," gives a detailed description of Paderewski's private Pullman car with its piano, library, heating system and telephone that was always connected to the local phone exchange. The reader is also appraised of Paderewski's meal and practicing schedule and of his special customs on concert days. From "Paderewski—Twentieth American Tour. Souvenir Program, Shrine Auditorium, Sunday Evening, April 2, 1939, L.E. Behymer Management." Collection of the Polish Music Center, USC
18 See Zamoyski, *Paderewski*, p. 126
19 See *Memoirs* by Paderewski and Lawton, p. 388-389
20 See Charles Phillips, *Paderewski—The Story of a Modern Immortal*, p. 156
21 See Eigeldinger, *Chopin: Pianist and Teacher*, p. 135-136
22 See Arthur Hedley, *Chopin*, p. 142
23 See Eigeldinger, *Chopin: Pianist and Teacher*, p. 181
24 Ibid., p. 138
25 Ibid., p. 139
26 Ibid., p. 276
27 Ibid., p. 277
28 Ibid., p. 277
29 Ibid., p. 276
30 Ibid., p. 267
31 Ibid., p. 270
32 Ibid., p. 294

33 See Charles Phillips, *Paderewski—The Story of a Modern Immortal*, p. 206
34 See Zamoyski, *Paderewski*, p. 246-250
35 See *Dzieje muzyki polskiej* [The History of Polish Music], p. 92
36 See Charles Phillips, *Paderewski—The Story of a Modern Immortal*, p. 200
37 Ibid., p. 162
38 Ibid., p. 162-164
39 Ibid., p. 208

CHAPTER FIVE

MUSIC OF CHOPIN AND PADEREWSKI

Chopin began to compose when he was seven years old; by the time he was fourteen, he already had a catalogue of a few Polonaises, a Military March and a Mazurka. His first published work, *Rondeau in C minor*, Op. 1, dates from 1825, when he was fifteen; his last composition, the Mazurka in F minor, Op. 68 no. 4 was written in 1849, the year he died at the age of thirty-nine. During the period of almost twenty-five years devoted to composing, Chopin produced some of the most beautiful and enduring repertoire that remains without doubt the highest achievement of Romantic era piano music. Chopin's position in the history of music is truly unique: his groundbreaking opus is revolutionary in terms of melody, harmony, and the use of distinctive piano textures, as well as classical in the supreme perfection of form and content that inhabit his music.

Paderewski too began to compose at a young age and his impulse to do so came from his fondness for improvising at the piano. Left mainly to his own devices by inadequate teachers, the childhood album of "Compositions of Ignace Paderewski" contained music he simply copied from the piano scores on hand:

[…] What interested me most when I started composing was that the calligraphic part of the composition should be beautiful, that it should look beautiful. Sound, I did not attach much importance to, then. I did not write music instinctively. I did it by comparison when looking at the piano music which I played myself. I followed the way it was printed, if you understand what I mean.[1]

Since this album of "compositions" has been lost, Paderewski's first extant work is his *Valse Mignonne*, dedicated to his teacher Gustaw Roguski, and written when Paderewski was sixteen. His Opus 1 consists of a *Prelude and*

Caprice and *Menuet in G minor*, also dating from 1876. Since his last work, Symphony in B minor, "Polonia," dates from 1907, Paderewski's activity as a composer lasted about thirty years.[2]

Although the composing careers of Chopin and Paderewski were of about the same duration, Chopin was a prolific author of a substantial body of music, while Paderewski's list of compositions is much less extensive. Since Chopin played in public only on rare occasions and divided his activities between teaching and composing, he had more time to write and perfect his works before introducing them to his public. Paderewski's case was quite different—most of his music was written during his student days in Warsaw, Berlin and Vienna. Once he began to perform and tour on a large scale in the 1890s, he found less and less time to compose. By the early 1900s Paderewski was basically trying to put the finishing touches on projects he had begun much earlier, including his opera *Manru*, the monumental Piano Sonata and Piano Variations, and finally, his Symphony in B minor. With a private performance of the Symphony in Lausanne on 26 December 1908 and its public premiere by the Boston Symphony Orchestra on 12 February 1909,

Paderewski's catalogue of compositions was closed. During the remaining thirty five years of his life, Paderewski concertized around the world, interrupting his pianistic career with a period of service to his country as a statesman during the years of World War I.

————————

Chopin's singular dedication to the piano—the instrument he understood intimately and played like no one else before or since—is among the greatest assets of his legacy. He was quite conscious of his extraordinary talent to compose for this medium and thus was able to give a free reign to his creative imagination. The luxurious sounds and coloristic effects Chopin drew from the piano inspired his contemporaries, left his public spellbound, and served as the foundation of music written by composers who followed him decades later, well into the twentieth century. Liszt's account of Chopin's importance as a composer is worthy of quoting; the two were cordial friends in Paris and Liszt genuinely admired Chopin's refined style and exceptional virtuosity. He also understood that Chopin's music pointed towards the future:

In making an analysis of the works of Chopin, we meet with beauties of a high order, expressions entirely new, and a harmonic tissue as original as erudite. In his compositions, boldness is always justified; richness, even exuberance, never interferes with clearness; singularity never degenerates into uncouth fantasticalness; the sculpturing is never disorderly; the luxury of ornament never overloads the chaste eloquence of the principal lines. His best works abound in combinations which may be said to form an epoch in the handling of musical style. Daring, brilliant and attractive, they disguise their profundity under so much grace, their science under so many charms, that it is with difficulty we free ourselves sufficiently from their magical enthrallment, to judge coldly of their theoretical value. Their worth has, however, already been felt; but it will be more highly estimated when the time arrives for a critical examination of the services rendered by them to art during that period of its course traversed by Chopin.[3]

It has been said that Chopin began composing with a Polonaise and ended with a Mazurka. It is so indeed, but the truth that hides behind this statement goes much deeper. The handful of Chopin's early Polonaises may share some traits with those composed by his predecessors like Ogiński or Szymanowska and are necessarily derivative of the prevailing and very popular models. Yet by the age of seventeen, when Chopin wrote his D minor Polonaise (published posthumously as Op. 71), he was already well on his own path of discovery and transformation of the genre. The heroic, epic, and patriotic note that many of the Polonaises

forcefully strike reflect Chopin's deep kinship with Poland's tragic fate during the dark years of partitions and uprisings. The weight of history evoked in Chopin's music was keenly felt by all those who became familiar with his Polonaises. Schumann's famous remark about "canon buried in flowers" is well known, but Liszt's insights into Chopin's patriotic sympathies are just as significant:

His Polonaises, characterized by an energetic rhythm, galvanize and electrify the torpor of indifference. The most noble traditional feelings of ancient Poland are embodied in them. The firm resolve and calm gravity of its men of other days breathe through these compositions. Generally of a martial character, courage and daring are rendered with that simplicity of expression, said to be a distinctive trait of this warlike people. They bring vividly before the imagination the ancient Poles, as we find them described in their chronicles; gifted with powerful organizations, subtle intellects, indomitable courage and earnest piety, mingled with high-born courtesy and a gallantry which never deserted them, whether on the eve of a battle, during its exciting course, in the triumph of victory, or amidst the gloom of defeat.[4]

In contrast to the Polonaises, Chopin's Mazurkas were his most original creations right from the early days of his composing career. The first of his fifty-six Mazurkas was written in 1824 and dedicated to his friend, Wilhelm Kolberg. It was most likely inspired by Chopin's experience of folk music

Figure 23: Chopin's Mazurka in A-flat major, Op. 7 no. 4, dating from 1824. Facsimile edition published by the Fryderyk Chopin Institute, Warsaw. Polish Music Center Archives

of Mazowsze (the region around Warsaw where he was born) and Kujawy (a region of north-central Poland where he spent summer vacations with friends). This short work— already containing some bold harmonies and modulations—was further refined by Chopin in Paris before it was published there as Op. 7 in 1832. Chopin's last Mazurka, written twenty-five years after his first, is an acutely introspective return to the sounds of Polish countryside from his youth.

Most importantly, Chopin's impact as a composer was first noticed through his highly idiomatic Mazurkas, which charmed the public and intrigued his fellow musicians. Hector Berlioz was one of them. After hearing Chopin in Paris, he was struck by the Mazurkas in particular, writing in *Le Rénovateur* in December of 1833:

[…] His melodies, all impregnated with Polish elements, have something naively untamed about them that charms and captivates by its very strangeness [...] Unfortunately, virtually nobody but Chopin himself can play his music and give it this unusual turn, this sense of the unexpected which is one of its principal beauties; his interpretation is shot through with a thousand nuances of movement of which he alone holds the secret, and which are impossible to convey by instructions. There are unbelievable details in his Mazurkas; and he has found how to render them doubly interesting by playing them with the utmost degree of softness, piano in the extreme, the hammers merely brushing the strings, so much so that one is tempted to go close to the instrument and put one's ear to it as if to a concert of sylphs or elves.[5]

Wilhelm von Lenz (1809-1883), who studied with Chopin for a few years in the 1840s, also commented on the uniquely patriotic mien of the Mazurkas:

Chopin's Mazurkas are the diary of his soul's journey through the socio-political territories of his Sarmatian dream-world! There his playing was truly at home; *in them resided* Chopin's originality as a pianist. He represented Poland, *the land of his dreams*, in the Parisian salons under Louis-Philippe—salons which *his* viewpoint allowed him to use as a political platform. Chopin was the *only political* pianist. He *incarnated* Poland, he *set* Poland to *music!*[6]

Just like the Mazurkas, Chopin's Etudes were another totally novel achievement. The two sets of twelve Etudes—Op. 10 and Op. 25—completely transformed the genre of a mechanical and musically unappealing exercise practiced by many composers who hoped to contribute to the improvement of piano technique standards. Under Chopin's poetic touch, the ferociously difficult passagework is but a stepping stone to the beautiful musical expression contained under the exploration of a particular pianistic challenge. The Op. 10 set, written by Chopin when he was only eighteen, is truly remarkable for the novelty of sounds and harmonies that are evoked as well as for the new pianistic textures. Berlioz observed that,

[…] In his Etudes one finds harmonic combinations of astonishing depth; he has created a kind of chromatic embroidery in several of his compositions, whose effect is so strange and piquant as to be impossible to describe.[7]

The second set of Etudes, written during the years 1832-1836 opened still new horizons in the art of piano playing. Chopin played Etudes from both opus numbers in his public and private recitals to the end of his life and, as this anonymous report in the 26 May 1834 issue of the *Neue Leipziger Zeitschrift für Musik* states, he did so effortlessly:

He played his Nocturnes and some of his Etudes. At a glance Chopin's scores look unplayable, so full are they of the most difficult figurations and chord formations; so one can only acknowledge him as a rare master when he plays them in such a way as to claim our complete wonderment. His playing is perfect in every respect. There we find tone, strength, infinite grace, sorrow, profound feeling, a cleanness and lightness in performance that leaves nothing more to wish for—and, most important of all, originality in his way of playing his multifariously original works. These all convey the impression of that youthful melancholy which every cultivated developing mind perceives. Where others sigh for love in nature, by hill and stream, Chopin composes instead; where others bring us to despair through their sorrowful sighing, he gladdens us. He is rightly the most beloved pianist.[8]

Chopin's Nocturnes, Impromptus, Preludes and the two self-standing works—the *Berceuse* and the *Barcarolle*—belong to the most romantic and graciously intimate music ever written, whose effect on the audience was magnetic. Tender melodies and languorous accompaniments in Chopin's twenty-one Nocturnes create an unmistakably personal atmosphere, akin to poetic narration. Nocturnes by John Field and Franz Schubert's Impromptus and *Moments musicaux* might have inspired Chopin's first attempts in this genre in the late 1820s. But his Op. 9 Nocturnes published in Paris in 1833 already show the hand of a master who expertly infused the admittedly simple formal layout of the Nocturne with a great wealth of consummate expression.

With their graceful arabesques and refined style, Chopin's Four Impromptus truly convey the impression of music created on the spot. The set of Twenty-four Preludes represents a collection of sparkling and miniature gems; some seem to be just sketches that capture a thought, an emotion, or a moment in time. In spite of their brevity they are fully self-contained and perfectly proportioned in their formal design.

The *Berceuse* and the *Barcarolle* are a variation on the nocturne principle. On top of the steadily recurring pattern in the left-hand, the delicate lace of right hand passagework in the *Berceuse* is astonishingly rich in colorful melodic turns. The magnificent *Barcarolle* with its luxurious harmonies and technically advanced passages that elicit the richest sonorities from the piano undoubtedly represents the apex of Chopin's lyrical achievement.

Chopin's Four Scherzos, the *Fantasie* in F minor, and Four Ballades represent another milestone in piano literature. Each breaks a new ground by defining its own genre. The Scherzo—a movement introduced by Beethoven in his Sonatas and Symphonies—becomes a much grander and more dramatic self-standing work in Chopin's interpretation of the well-defined canon. Built on widely differing dramatic premises, each Scherzo follows its own logic of expression and form. The extraordinary drama of the B-minor Scherzo is offset by its middle section, where Chopin inserted a well-known melody of one of the most touching Polish Christmas carols, *Lulajże Jezuniu* [Sleep Baby Jesus]. According to Wilhelm von Lenz, Chopin's playing of this section "produced an indescribable impression."[9] The Second Scherzo, with its rhetorical opening motive, makes for a very arresting opening:

I saw Chopin dwell at length on this bar and again at each of its reappearances. 'That's the key to the whole piece,' he would say.[10]

The soaring melody that follows the opening theme also required great care in execution:

Chopin was just as exacting over the simple quaver accompaniment of the cantilena, as well as the cantilena itself: 'You should think of [Giuditta] Pasta, of Italian song! – not of French Vaudeville,' he said one day with more than a touch of irony.[11]

The Third Scherzo is the tersest and most virtuosic of the four, with its main subject clad in a torrent of stern octaves. The contrasting chorale theme is solemn and distinct, but also receives a most delicate ornamentation of cascading passages in the upper regions of the keyboard. The Fourth Scherzo is a radical departure from its predecessors: cast in the sunny key of E major, it has the smiling demeanor of a caprice basking among the gentle waves of gossamer staccato chords and trills.

The *Fantasie* in F minor occupies the middle ground between the Scherzos and the Ballades by fusing elements from each into its design. It is a very ambitious work built upon several strongly contrasting subjects that add up to a dark and mighty pianistic *tour de force*. With their abstract yet strongly-evoked narrative the Ballades successfully combine poetic expression with paramount virtuosity. Although quite different in character, the *Fantasie* and the Ballades clearly share the same common denominator of an impassioned musical declamation. The French novelist and playwright, Félicien Mallefille,[12] remembered the impact of Chopin's G minor Ballade:

Some time ago, in one of those soirees where, surrounded by select and sympathetic hearers, you give full rein to your inspiration, you let us hear that Polish Ballade, which we love so much. When you had finished we remained silent and pensive, still hearing the sublime song whose last note had long vanished into space… What thought had the melodious voice of your piano awakened in us? I cannot say; for each one sees in music, as in clouds, different things.[13]

Over a dozen of Chopin's published Waltzes as well as at least five posthumously published ones offer quite a different portrait of their composer.[14] They all are full of charm and grace, dash and, on several occasions, sparkling humor. Building on the existing Viennese tradition, Chopin once again elevated the genre of the Waltz to a new level of sophistication and elegance. He was clearly fond of the dance which he first witnessed in the aristocratic salons of Warsaw and later encountered in Vienna:

Among the numerous pleasure of Vienna the hotel evenings are famous. During supper Strauss or Lanner play waltzes; [...] After every waltz they get huge applause; and if they play a *Quodlibet*, or jumble of opera, song and dance, the hearers are so overjoyed that they don't know what to do with themselves. It shows the corrupt taste of the Viennese public. I wanted to send you a waltz that I have composed, but it is late now; you shall have it afterwards. I don't send

mazurkas because they are not copied yet; they are not for dancing.[15]

Chopin's Waltzes are much more sophisticated then their Viennese predecessors. Occasionally, beneath their exuberant exterior there are also moments of repose and melancholy.[16] Just like the Preludes, Etudes and Nocturnes, Chopin programmed his Waltzes in concerts throughout his life.

Chopin wrote only three piano sonatas and each of them inhabits a world of its own. The first, Op. 4, dating from 1827, is a student work with many interesting Beethovenian touches. As such, this Sonata represents perhaps the single instance of Chopin's music that is rarely heard on concert stages. It was first published in 1851, two years after Chopin's death. The Second Sonata in B-flat minor (1839) is well-known—and most often performed—perhaps because of its famous Funeral March that serves as the third movement. This March was, in fact, written two years earlier and it provided Chopin with seeds of inspiration for the surrounding movements. In spite of the initial puzzlement from various quarters (including Schumann who completely misunderstood this work), the B-flat minor Sonata presents a superb company of four diverse movement that with magnificent resolve carry the dramatic narrative all the way through to the end. The Finale is one of the most unusual closing statements in all of music history—a fleeting and dark impression of hushed unisons in the lower register of the piano that serve as a grim counterpart to the Funeral March that preceded it. Chopin shared some insights on this work in an August 1839 letter posted from Nohant and addressed to his friend in Paris, Julian Fontana:

> Here I am writing a Sonata in B-flat minor, containing the march that you know. There is an allegro, then a Scherzo E-flat minor, the march and a short finale, perhaps 3 of my pages; the left hand in unison with the right, gossiping after the march.[17]

The Third Piano Sonata is the grandest and perhaps the most complex. Written in 1844 it is a product of Chopin's maturity and it possesses an astonishing wealth of melodic ideas that are set into a grand formal design. The first movement's stern opening motive and the cantilena of the second subject are unsurpassed in their dramatic juxtaposition. Densely polyphonic textures of the development and a splendid recapitulation followed by an effective coda cap this majestic movement. The following Scherzo is driven by the contrast of fleeting passagework with a noble and quiet chorale. The slow movement is the equivalent of a gently flowing aria which, when played by Chopin to Marie Roubaud during her lesson, "had his pupil in tears."[18] The splendid Finale with two contrasting themes exploring pathos and virtuosity closes the Sonata with an extended and truly brilliant final summary.

Although small in number, Chopin's chamber music and compositions for piano and orchestra also merit attention. His works for cello and piano in particular offer a fascinating study of Chopin's development as a composer. The *Introduction et Polonaise* is a brilliant salon piece resulting from Chopin's friendship with the Radziwiłł family. Prince Antoni was a cellist and a composer; his daughter, Wanda, a good pianist and Chopin gave her a few piano lessons. The Polonaise was written for the father-daughter duet in 1829, but the Introduction was added a few years later.[19] Chopin's subsequent work for cello and piano, the *Grand Duo* for Cello and Piano, was written in Paris in 1832 jointly by Chopin and his cellist friend, Auguste Franchomme. This friendship led to their collaborative concerts in the 1830s and 1840s and culminated with the premiere of Chopin's Sonata for Cello and Piano at Chopin's final concert in Paris in February of 1848.[20] It was Chopin's last large-scale work and its monumental scale and advanced harmonic language are astonishingly prophetic of music that was written over a half a century later. Chopin's only other noteworthy chamber music composition is his Piano Trio. Completed in 1829, this work was also closely connected to the Radziwiłłs since Chopin worked on it during his visits with the family. It is a graceful four-movement piece with a very complex piano part that fully reflects the extent of Chopin's youthful virtuosity. Its piano writing style recalls the *Polish Fantasy* and *Rondo à la Krakowiak*, two glittering pieces for piano and orchestra composed approximately at the same time.

Chopin's two Piano Concertos were written during his last two years in Warsaw. The F minor Concerto dates from 1829 and the E minor from 1830. Hearing Hummel perform in Warsaw in 1828 and being familiar with piano concertos by early Romantic (and now forgotten) composers like Field, Ries, or Kalkbrenner, undoubtedly provided Chopin with some ideas how to begin. He followed his predecessors by writing fairly conventional orchestral *tutti* sections but as soon as the soloist's turn came, a wholly new personality emerged. After the success of the *Don Giovanni Variations* for piano and orchestra in 1827, Chopin knew quite well how to write effective passagework for the soloist. Since at the same time he was composing his first Etudes and completing the Piano Trio, Chopin poured the joy of creating a work tailored to his virtuosity into these two grand essays for piano and orchestra. The slow middle movements of both Concertos are remarkable for their tenderness and maturity, with several breathtaking touches of orchestral color and most inventive solo piano writing. The opening movements of both Concertos combine a sense of majesty, noble pathos and grand seriousness; the closing movements on the other hand are a riot of bravura passagework cast in the whirlwind form of Polish folk dances—the mazurka in the Finale of the F minor Concerto and the *krakowiak* in the E minor.

Wilhelm von Lenz witnessed how Chopin taught the E minor Concerto to his best student, a child prodigy from Transylvania, Carl Filtsch (1830-1845):

[…] He played us the themes indescribably beautifully and gave us hints for playing the runs and passagework. He wanted the runs *cantabile*, with a certain measure of strength and bravura within, trying to bring out as much as possible the slightest thematic fragments, using the most delicate touch, even where the runs are no more than runs—which in this piece is the exception. […] Filtsch studied the work with Chopin solo section by solo section; he was never allowed to play the movement right through, since it would affect Chopin too powerfully; Chopin maintained besides that the entire work's power was contained within each solo section. […] When at last Filtsch was allowed to play the whole movement—an occasion for which he had prepared himself by Roman Catholic fasting and prayer as well as by reading the score under Chopin's direction (practicing had been forbidden)—Chopin said, 'Now this movement is sufficiently "in place" for us to play it: I'll be your orchestra.' […] With his incomparable way of accompanying, Chopin evoked all the ingenious and elusive qualities of the orchestration. He played from memory. I have never heard anything comparable to that first *tutti* as he played it himself at the piano. As for the lad, he worked marvels. It was the experience of a lifetime.[21]

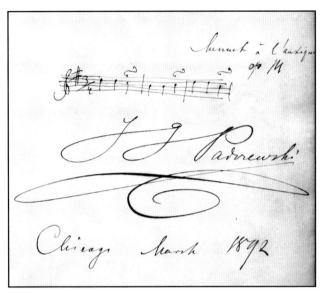

Figure 24: The opening bars of Paderewski's famous *Menuet*, Op. 14. The Paso Robles Collection, Polish Music Center, USC.

The three decades of Paderewski's career devoted to composing yielded a broad range of music in forms small and large and of generally variable quality. Some of Paderewski's compositions were extremely popular in his lifetime and closely matched his fame as a pianist. This was certainly the case of his *Menuet* Op. 14, the opening bars of which were literally on the lips of multitudes. Audiences at Paderewski's concerts often demanded it for an encore and applauded with approval as soon as he began to play it. A Spanish border official hummed the *Menuet's* main tune as soon as he recognized the elderly Paderewski, who was travelling from Switzerland through France and Spain to Portugal in 1940 on his way to the United States.[22] But many other compositions—including Paderewski's Symphony, the opera *Manru*, and as a number of his piano works—practically vanished from the repertoire after his death in 1941.

A paradox of Paderewski's career in music is that during his young years he was seriously encouraged by many of his teachers to pursue composition. Many of them felt that a man in his early twenties was already too old to succeed as a touring virtuoso. Consequently, Paderewski dutifully studied composition but always looked for ways of finding an avenue of becoming a concert pianist.

From the beginning, even at the Conservatory, everything was against me—discouragement on all sides. Even those who were my intimate friends looked upon virtuosity as something inferior. As I was at that time very fond of composing, and some of my first compositions were rather noteworthy in that little circle of friends, I almost lost myself any hope of becoming a successful pianist. So naturally I turned then to composition.[23]

He wrote a number of short piano pieces that clearly show a sensitive musician with a good ear for melody and fresh ideas that may have come from improvising at the piano, something—according to Helena Modjeska—Paderewski clearly enjoyed as a young man:

He used to come often to our villa, and it was impossible to keep him away from the piano. Sometimes he played long after midnight, and had to be taken from the instrument by force when the refreshments were announced.[24]

However as soon as Paderewski succeeded in conquering the greatest concert stages of Europe and North America as a concert pianist, his composition activities had to be drastically curtailed. With the passage of time Paderewski's heavy touring schedule and constant practicing led to episodes of nervous tension that made him very averse to the piano. Looking for an exit from concertizing, Paderewski returned to writing music. After some of his large-scale works were premiered in major venues of Europe and America in the early 1900s, critics and music writers expressed hope that Paderewski may still become more widely known as a composer.[25] Others reacted to the performances of Paderewski's music by expressing regret that his career as a soloist was over. At the time of Paderewski's opera, *Manru,* was premiered in Dresden, Paderewski was also performing there:

During my stay in Dresden—we are still in 1901—I had to play in one orchestra concert given for the benefit of the Opera orchestra. I played no better and no worse than usual, but as my opera was in rehearsal, some of the local critics found many faults with my playing, and were evidently very glad to air their opinions. They were full of complaints and criticism. "What a pity," one paper commented, "that Paderewski is now composing, for he is no more a great pianist." Another critic wrote even more strongly. He said, "It is to be deeply regretted that Paderewski's time is now being devoted to composition, because his piano playing is being neglected and evidence of this neglect was very manifest at his concert yesterday," and so on. Ah, well, it was human nature.[26]

Just as in the oeuvre of Chopin, piano was the main focus for Paderewski's creative efforts. Undoubtedly inspired by Chopin's Mazurkas, Preludes, Impromptus and Nocturnes, Paderewski began to try his hand in similar small-scale forms for his first piano compositions. Before he was twenty, Paderewski had a portfolio that included *Prelude and Caprice* coupled with the *Menuet in G minor* listed as Op. 1, *Gavotte in E minor*, *Mélodie in C major*, and *Valse Mélancolique*, published as Op. 2, as well as three other piano pieces without opus numbers: *Impromptu in F major*, *Intermezzo in G minor*, and *Intermezzo in C minor*. The years 1880-1886 brought a number of new piano compositions arranged in collections of several titles each. *Chants du Voyageur*, Op. 8 (dedicated to Helena Górska who many years later became Paderewski's second wife), is a cycle of five charming pieces, of which the third is a well-known *Mélodie in B major*. The opening bars of this short piece are a distant echo of the middle section of Chopin's First Scherzo. The great German violinist Joseph Joachim was an early admirer of this lovely piece:

> […] Joachim invited me to play a few of my own compositions which I of course did without hesitation. A small collection of short piano pieces published under the title, which I never liked, "Chants du Voyageur," was selected for that purpose. The third piece in it (in B Major) seemed to impress Joachim quite particularly—and to such an extent that he asked me to repeat it several times. In general the impressions these compositions made upon him was extremely encouraging to me.[27]

Polish folklore inspired many of Paderewski's early piano pieces. The *Krakowiak*, Op. 3, was followed by Three Polish Dances Op. 5 (*Krakowiak* in E major, Mazurka in C minor, and *Krakowiak* in B-flat minor), and still more Polish Dances, Op. 9 (three Mazurkas, two *Krakowiaks* and a Polonaise). Paderewski was greatly helped in having his compositions published by the prestigious firm of Bote & Bock[28] so early in his career. Maurycy Moszkowski, a brilliant Polish pianist and composer then living in Berlin, helped Paderewski to find a publisher:

> I was introduced to Mr. Bock by a very fine man and good musician who enjoyed much popularity. His name was Mortiz Moszkowski, and it was through this introduction of Moszkowski's that my compositions were published, because it was extremely difficult, being young and unknown, to find a publisher. He, Bock,

gave me for those first compositions (about nine pieces) the enormous sum of 200 marks, that was about $50. You know I never really expected that—he acted very generously under the circumstances.[29]

Since Paderewski's publisher was one of the most important figures in Berlin's musical circles, his house attracted all kinds of notable musicians. This is how the young Polish composer was introduced to Anton Rubinstein:

[…] I went to dinner and there I met that great, that immense artist. He was most agreeable and gracious and after dinner he came to me and said, "I hear a great deal about your compositions from Mr. Bock, who speaks highly of them, and I should like to hear some tonight. Will you not play me something?" I had just finished a set off Variations, which I then played for him, and he was very pleased. He listened attentively. "You have a brilliant future," he said when I had finished. "Now play me something more, something else—play some short pieces." I did so, and again he was very complimentary, very kind. "You should compose more," he went on, "more for the piano." Oh, I protested, "I cannot really do much for the piano, I play so little myself." "Nonsense," he replied, "you should play more, I tell you. You have an inborn technique and you could have, I am sure, a splendid pianistic career." Those fateful words of his left me almost stunned for the moment. I did not know how to answer him—it overwhelmed me. It was such a surprise. This experience with Rubinstein had a tremendous effect. What he said changed my world completely.[30]

Other piano pieces from Paderewski's fertile imagination soon followed. When he studied in Vienna with Leschetizky, Paderewski was introduced to Leschetizky's second wife, Annette Essipov, a brilliant pianist and a charming individual. She was quite keen to play Paderewski's piano music, and he dedicated the set of five piano pieces—*Album de Mai: Scènes romantiques pour piano*, Op. 10—to his beloved teacher's wife. Another set, *Album tatrzańskie* [Tatra Album], Op. 12 was a collection that served as a musical souvenir of Paderewski's sojourns in the Tatra mountain resort town of Zakopane in the south of Poland. This set exists in two versions—for piano 4-hands and for piano solo and is dedicated to Dr. Tytus Chałubiński. Paderewski's set of Variations and Fugue in A minor—an ambitious early work from 1883 that was published by Bock in Berlin in 1885 and dedicated to pianist Eugène d'Albert—was another of Paderewski's works that Annette Essipov performed on many occasions, helping Paderewski to gain more recognition as a composer.

Paderewski composed yet another set of short piano pieces in 1884. His *Humoresques de Concert pour piano* Op. 14 were a more ambitious undertaking, since the six pieces that comprise the cycle are divided into two sections, *A l'antique* and *A la moderne*, with three compositions written on each theme. The first three are a studied pastiche and their titles provide clues to the composer's source of inspiration in keyboard literature of the past: *Menuet*, *Sarabande*, and *Caprice*. Paderewski's famous *Menuet* that opens the set began with a "musical joke" he played on two of his elderly gentleman friends—Dr. Tytus Chałubiński and writer Alexander Świętochowski—who "worshipped" Mozart:

Mozart was their God and they would listen to nothing else. Finally I got tired of it and I determined to put an end to it. I had an idea. One day returning to the house of Kerntopf, where I stayed in Warsaw, I sat down at the piano and improvised a minuet! Just for fun. [...] of course the Minuet was quite different from what it is now, it was far simpler. It was devoid of any ornament, purely Mozart in style, without the ending cadenza. That was added later. [...] The good doctor! He was eagerly awaiting my arrival and asked as usual for some music, would I not play a little Mozart for him? [...] Almost before I finished the last bar the dear old man was on his feet. "Oh, Mozart," he cried. "What a wonderful piece! Tell me, Paderewski, is there any one now alive who could write such music?" I looked at him, and then I said, "Yes, there is such a person. *I have!*" [...] It was a terrible blow to them and they were very angry at first at being so misled. Naturally it ended our Mozart for that evening, but a few nights later I was asked to play the real Mozart, which I did with pleasure and a good deal of remorse. And then they asked very politely afterwards to hear the Minuet. Ah! It was a touching moment for us all. I played it for them feeling very penitent by that time, and they expressed themselves as liking it very much. In fact, they became

so fond of it that I always had to play it for them, and then I realized that this piece was going to make my name popular—it will help me in my career, I thought. And such was the case, for it was that same Minuet that so pleased Leschetizky when I returned for the second time to Vienna. It was a revelation to him.[31]

The other three pieces in Op. 14 are miniatures in the "modern style," and include *Burlesque*, *Intermezzo polacco*, and *Cracovienne fantastique*. Of these, the last is perhaps the most famous and most innovative; a sprightly theme and lively piano passagework with good-natured humor make it a concert favorite to this day. Paderewski recorded both the *Menuet* and the *Cracovienne fantastique* from Op. 14, giving a valuable insight to what he expected these pieces to sound like under the hands of a Romantic-era virtuoso.

Another fine set of piano pieces is represented by the six *Miscellanea pour Piano*, written around 1888. The opening *Légende* in A-flat major is somewhat reminiscent of Chopin's Ballade in the same key, but is much shorter and simpler in terms of its overall form. The *Mélodie* in G-flat major is another short but beautiful piece and the Nocturne in B-flat major—the only work of Paderewski with this title—is an effective and truly heartfelt composition. Variations in A-major that are also in this set are less-well known, but feature quite a challenge for the performer.

Paderewski also wrote some chamber music and these compositions, although rarely performed, merit much more attention from modern performers. The Sonata for Violin and Piano, Op. 13, is dedicated to the famous violin virtuoso, Pablo de Sarasate. It is a surprisingly mature and accomplished work from the barely twenty-year old composer. The first movement features fine writing for the duet with many demanding and effective passages for piano and violin. The second, rhapsodic movement is full of humor and whimsy, equally distributing the musical material between the two partners. The finale is a fine example of ardently romantic music, abounding in dazzling material for the violin and piano. Nicely proportioned in its duration of about twenty-five minutes it makes a perfect recital piece, something that Brahms noticed right away:

I remember well the opinion that he expressed about the Sonata for Piano and Violin which was at a later meeting of that club. When he heard it he listened attentively as always, and then he said, "Well, Paderewski, it is very effective, very fine, but it is not chamber music; it is a concert Sonata." That was a little criticism and a valuable one, I thought. At the same time it was also a kind of appreciation. […][32]

Having heard a few compliments from one of the greatest living composers, Paderewski immediately thought of studying with him. After all, his piano teacher, Leschetizky, was on friendly terms with Brahms, and Paderewski thought a little advice on composing could be very helpful to him:

Brahms lived in Vienna and I saw him very often during my stay there. […] I approached him on one occasion with the purpose of asking him whether he would perhaps give me a few lessons. But he would not consider it. "No," he said. "No. I never teach. I have no time. And besides, you do not need further tuition. You can become your own teacher now. You do not need me." His refusal, however, was a very real disappointment to me.[33]

The remainder of Paderewski's chamber music catalogue is represented by three cycles of songs. Here Paderewski continued the tradition of setting music to Polish Romantic-era poets, a path that was laid for him by Maria Szymanowska, Frederic Chopin and Stanisław Moniuszko. Paderewski's Four Songs, Op. 7, were written to texts by Adam Asnyk, a celebrated Polish poet whom the composer befriended through Helena Modjeska and Tytus Chałubiński in Zakopane during the summer of 1884. A few years later, Paderewski completed a cycle of *Six Songs to words by Adam Mickiewicz*, the most important Polish poet of the Romantic era. Mickiewicz had settled in Paris shortly after Chopin's arrival there. The two were close friends and Chopin often provided an *ex tempore* accompaniment to Mickiewicz's improvised verse during joint performances for Polish émigrés in Paris. For all Poles, Mickiewicz was a national bard and an important Polish patriot, whose poetry was especially relevant to all Polish exiles. Franz Liszt, who occasionally came to such soirees in Paris, described Mickiewicz as:

Dark and silent, apart from all others, fell the motionless profile of Mickiewicz: the Dante of the North, he seemed always to find "the salt of the stranger bitter, and his steps hard to mount."[34]

Paderewski's last venture in the genre of chamber music was another set of songs for voice and piano, *Douze melodies sur de poésies de Catulle Mèndes* that were completed in 1903:

Within a fortnight I also wrote twelve French songs to the words of Catulle Mèndes. Madame Modjeska and her husband were staying here at Morges then, and every evening I played a new song to her. It was a happy time.[35]

Like numerous nineteenth-century virtuosos, Paderewski wrote works for piano and orchestra and used them as vehicles for building his credentials as a composer as well as a travelling virtuoso. Here too, Paderewski was following the example of Chopin who, in addition to two piano concertos wrote four extended pieces for piano and orchestra, the *Don Giovanni Variations*, *Polish Fantasy*, *Rondo à la Krakowiak*, and *Andante spianato and Grand Polonaise Brillante*. Paderewski however managed to complete only two works for piano and orchestra: the Concerto for Piano and Orchestra in A minor, Op. 17 and the *Polish Fantasy*, Op. 19. Paderewski's Concerto was first sketched out in Vienna, just as he began to study with Leschetizky:

[…] I had started writing that concerto in '88. After the first season in Paris I wrote it, in a very short time. I scored it in '89 in Paris and wanted to play it myself, but Madame Essipov said, as she had introduced some of my composition already in Vienna, she would like to do this concerto too. As Leschetizky had invited the great conductor, Hans Richter, to hear this composition, she was naturally anxious to play it.[36]

When the Concerto was ready, Paderewski sought advice of many fellow musicians, including the distinguished French pianist and composer Camille Saint-Saëns, regarding the merits of his new work. After hearing it in private solo performance by Paderewski, Saint-Saëns quickly reassured the young

Polish composer that he had nothing to worry about. The concerto was premiered in Vienna by Madame Essipov, and the orchestra was conducted by Hans Richter. This three-movement work is quite original in its thematic material and very inventive in the orchestral accompaniment. The piano writing is transparent and effective and the orchestral part is skillfully scored. For a work of a young composer still in his mid twenties, it was a very auspicious beginning, demonstrating Paderewski's gifts as a composer and pianist. The Concerto was well received right from the start:

> [...] So it was Madame Essipov who played my Concerto for the first time a few days after Richter read the score, and it had an immediate success. [...] It was favorably received, not only by the audience but by the critics as well.

Afterwards, Paderewski performed his Concerto on many occasions, including his debut in America in November of 1891. With Walter Damrosch conducting the orchestra, Paderewski began the evening with Saint-Saëns's Fourth Piano Concerto and finished the program with his own Piano Concerto. The distinguished New York critic, James Huneker, found the interpretation of Saint-Saëns's Concerto "totally overwhelming" and Paderewski's Concerto a work of genius, with the impression of the debut evening "a success that was stupendous."[37]

Polish Fantasia for Piano and Orchestra was a product of a happy and restful holiday Paderewski spent with his son, family and friends on the French coast:

> In the summer of that year, 1893, I was living with my boy and some friends in a quiet little place in Normandy called Yport. For the first time in my arduous career in foreign countries, I could invite some people dear to my heart to spend a few weeks with me. My sister came to stay with me, and I was glad to have also my dear old friend Edward Kerntopf. I felt very happy then. It was a holiday time. [...] I was free. I began to compose again. I started a composition, a "Polish Fantasia," for piano and orchestra, which I finished within five weeks. That Fantasia was performed by myself for the first time at the Festival of Norwich, England, under the conductorship of Mr. Randegger, a fine teacher of singing and an excellent conductor, and it met with considerable success. It was also performed in the same season (by myself) in London with Georg Heschel, who was then conducting many orchestral concerts. Afterwards it was played by several noted artists.[38]

The 4 October 1893 premiere of the *Polish Fantasia* elicited excellent press reviews, including the following notice in the *London Sunday Times*:

> The new Fantasia proved to be a symphonic poem for piano and orchestra in four movements (not three, as stated in the analysis), and a thoroughly well thought-

out musicianly work to boot. Its chief characteristics are its intense national feeling, its constructive skill, and its enormous difficulty. The themes are all original, and it takes a quick ear to perceive on first hearing with what skill the whole of them are derived or developed from two or three main subjects. The bold introductory passages merge imperceptibly into the well-worked *allegro moderato*; the impetuous scherzo, with its mazurka-like rhythm, brings a great change, but in the *andante* (a gem of dreamy, plaintive melody), the composer is in reality metamorphosing material from his *allegro*; while the finale, after starting with a dashing *Cracovienne*, obtains its most grandiose effect from the theme of the scherzo, given here in augmentation.[39]

In the early 1900s, after another decade-long interlude of intense travel and concertizing, Paderewski once again decided to rest and return to composing. His personal and professional life had settled down, at least for the time being, and he had several compositional projects that needed to be completed. The most challenging was the opera that he began sketching out shortly after the premiere of his *Polish Fantasia*:

> [...] A Polish writer and poet, Alfred Nossig by name, had approached me repeatedly with a proposition for writing a book for an opera. So, out of several outlines suggested, I selected one which was afterward written for me. That book, though not then in its definite form, was sent to me toward the end of 1893 and became the libretto for my opera, *Manru*.[40]

The piano-vocal draft of the score was ready in 1895, but since Paderewski was touring, the completion of this project took several more years.[41] The opera, based on the novel *Chata za wsią* [A Shack Outside a Village] by Józef Ignacy Kraszewski, is a story of love between a free-spirited gypsy and his peasant girl bride. Since both are outcasts in their respective communities, a tragic ending is inevitable. *Manru* was premiered on 29 May 1901 in Dresden with the Polish premiere following in Lwów on 8 June 1901. New York's Metropolitan Opera presented the American premiere on 14 February 1902. The reviews were generally favorable, but the libretto was criticized and the opera has been heard only very rarely since then.[42]

Seeking a place where he could compose in peace, in 1899 Paderewski acquired a large house near Morges, Switzerland, and moved there permanently. Having established himself as very successful virtuoso, he was still trying to make his mark as a composer:

> We are now approaching the year 1903, the most important year in my activity as a composer. [...] I decided then to stop playing for a year and write something. So in 1903 I remained almost the entire year at Morges, and began to compose. First of all I wrote my Piano Sonata, which is one of my important and best works. But it is extremely difficult and for that reason will never be very popular.
> The second work was the completion of my third set of Variations, which I had begun years before while still in Strasbourg. I had retained only a few of the variations from that period, so I wrote a series of new ones ending

with the fugue. This work is my best piano composition, I think. It is extremely difficult and perhaps too long, but it contains quite a few things which were then almost a revelation in their character and novelty.

[...] After that I wrote a sketch of my Symphony. That took several months. The orchestration, however, was done several years later. That composition was written in commemoration of the last Polish revolution of 1863. It was the fortieth anniversary.[43]

Paderewski's Piano Sonata in E-flat minor, Op. 21, is a grand and serious composition. Rarely performed, it is a work of considerable beauty and difficulty, challenging both the pianist and the audience to an incandescently romantic and darkly brilliant *tour de force*. Its three movements are carefully balanced and adhere to classical sonata forms. With its forward-surging themes, the mood of the opening *Allegro con fuoco* is agitated and passionate, with both virtuosic and lyrical elements vying for the listener's attention. The following *Andante ma non troppo* movement, with its lilting 6/8 main subject, dwells mostly within the boundaries of a romantic *canzona*. The closing *Allegro vivace* movement is launched decisively, in a *toccata* style. The bass line recalls the opening theme of the first movement, and this figure is eventually transformed into an extensive fugato section. The Sonata's concluding movement scales the heights of noble and fine climaxes, providing one of the most satisfying finales since Chopin's and Liszt's essays in the same form. Paderewski premiered the work on 26 April 1907 at the Royal Academy of Music in London and programmed it frequently in recitals during the following season.

Just like the Sonata, whose early sketches date back to Paderewski's studies in Vienna in the late 1880s, some of the material in the Variations in E-flat minor, Op. 23, also comes from the same period. Paderewski's previous two sets of Variations—Op. 11 and Op. 16—were written in the mid 1880s and this last set builds upon the previous attempts at the variation form. Many reviewers noted similarities in Paderewski's last set of variations to Chopin's Etudes; indeed his twenty variations explore a wide variety of piano textures and technical challenges. A magnificent fugue closes this monumental late Romantic work. Paderewski premiered the Variations on 28 February 1907 at a recital in Bristol, England and programmed it occasionally afterwards.

Although Paderewski began to work on his only Symphony in 1903, he did not finish it until 1908 and the work was first heard on 12 February 1909:

[...] My tour finished in 1908, and then Mr. Ellis, who heard that I had written a symphony, asked that its first performance in America be given with the Boston Symphony Orchestra. That proposition appealed to me greatly, but it also meant extra hard work to orchestrate the Symphony, which was yet to be done. Together with that proposal came another invitation to play as soloist in all the concerts where my Symphony was to be performed by the Boston Orchestra, to make another little tour in America, the tour to begin in December, 1908. I accepted with pleasure, of course. It was most gratifying.

Then I returned to Europe. Again I played concerts in Paris and in London, and again at those distinguished yearly musicals of Mrs. Astor. And then I started the orchestration of my Symphony, which was finished toward the end of November. I worked tremendously.

In December I returned to America and first played in several recitals. Then my Symphony was performed in Boston, and afterward in New York, Washington, Philadelphia, and Baltimore, and it was well received by the public as well as the critics.[44]

The work on the Symphony exhausted Paderewski, and he was forced to stop his tour and try all sorts of treatments for his nerves and his tired hands. As it turned out, his massive Symphony in B minor, *Polonia*, Op. 24, would be his valedictorian gesture as a composer. With seventy-five minutes of brooding and expansive music, Paderewski made his final farewell to his ambitions as a composer. Another three decades of worldwide appearances as a concert pianist and an interlude on the world stage of politics still lay ahead.

1. See Paderewski and Lawton, *Memoirs*, p. 17

2. Paderewski composed a short patriotic march for chorus with piano accompaniment in 1917, *Hej Orle biały* [Onwards, White Eagle], which is his final composition.

3. See Franz Liszt, *Life of Chopin*, p. 5

4. Ibid., p. 14-15

5. See Jean-Jacques Eigeldinger, *Chopin: Pianist and Teacher*, p. 71

6. Ibid., p. 71

7. Ibid., p. 272

8. Ibid., p. 291

9. Ibid., p. 84

10. Ibid., p. 85

11. Ibid., p. 85

12. Jean Pierre Félicien Mallefille (1813-1868) was George Sand's lover and a friend of Chopin until he learned of Chopin's relationship with Sand. On 9 September 1838 he published a well-considered article about Chopin's music in the *Revue et Gazette Musicale*. Shortly thereafter Sand broke up her relationship with Mallefille and left Paris in mid-October. Travelling separately a few weeks later, Chopin joined Sand in Perpignan in the south of France. By early November Chopin and Sand were steaming from Barcelona towards their holiday in Mallorca.

13. See Arthur Hedley, *Chopin*, p. 186-187

14. At least six of Chopin's Waltzes written during the years 1826-1830 are now lost. The only indication of their existence is a catalogue of unpublished manuscripts that Chopin's sister, Ludwika, made before they were lost in an apartment fire caused by the Russian military in Warsaw in 1863.

15. See *Chopin's Letters*, p. 129

16. Chopin himself described the A minor Waltz Op. 34 as *Valse mélancolique*. See Jean-Jacques Eigeldinger, *Chopin: Pianist and Teacher*, p. 86.

17. See *Chopin's Letters*, p. 204

18. Ibid., p. 61

19. The Introduction was written in 1830 and published together with the Polonaise in 1833. The work is dedicated to the principal cellist of Vienna's Royal Opera, Joseph Merk. Chopin befriended Merk during his second visit in the Austrian capital.

20. Only the second, third and the fourth movement of Chopin's Cello Sonata were played by Chopin and Franchomme at the Salle Pleyel concert on 16 February 1848. With the violinist Jean-Delphin Alard, Franchomme and Chopin also performed a piano trio by Mozart. Chopin also played his *Berceuse*, *Barcarolle*, and the Waltz in D-flat major, Op. 64, among other solo pieces.

21. See Jean-Jacques Eigeldinger, *Chopin: Pianist and Teacher*, p. 66-67

22. See Aniela Strakacz, *Paderewski as I Knew Him*, p. 291

23. See Paderewski and Lawton, *Memoirs*, p. 59

24. See Helena Modjeska, *Memoirs and Impressions*, p. 464-468

25. Edward Algernon Baughan in his book *Ignaz Jan Paderewski* wrote: "Paderewski has certainly more originality than Rubinstein, and as he is now only in his forty-seventh year there is every possibility that he will make a name for himself as composer." (p. 78)

26 See Paderewski and Lawton, *Memoirs*, p. 309

27 Ibid., p. 65

28 Bote & Bock is a music publishing firm, founded in Berlin in 1838 by Eduard Bote and Gustav Bock. It remained in the Bock family until 1935.

29 See Paderewski and Lawton, *Memoirs*, p. 63

30 Ibid., p 63-64

31 Ibid., p. 109-111

32 Ibid., p. 91

33 Ibid., p. 92

34 See Franz Liszt, *Life of Chopin*, p. 65

35 See Paderewski and Lawton, *Memoirs*, p. 327

36 Ibid., p. 120

37 See Adam Zamoyski, *Paderewski*, p. 66

38 See Paderewski and Lawton, *Memoirs*, p. 267

39 See Henry T. Finck, *Paderewski and His Art*, p. 41. Whittingham & Atherton, New York 1895

40 See Paderewski and Lawton, *Memoirs*, p. 268

41 In his *Memoirs*, Paderewski wrote, "These tours, of course, put an end to my work on the opera. The opera, alas, was now enjoying a long rest! It could not be otherwise. You see I was obligated to begin playing again. I needed money. My ten fingers were my fortune." (p. 273)

42 *Manru* was staged again in Poland recently, recorded live and released by DUX Records in Poland.

43 See Paderewski and Lawton, *Memoirs*, p. 326-327

44 Ibid., p. 371

~ CHAPTER SIX ~

PRIVATE LIVES

A comparison of the domestic lives of Chopin and Paderewski yields many fascinating parallels. Both divided their lives almost equally between Poland and a French-speaking country. Chopin was twenty when he left Warsaw in 1830 and spent the remaining nineteen years of his life in Paris. Paderewski was close to forty when he finally decided to pull his roots out of Poland and for the next four decades resided on the outskirts of Lausanne in the French-speaking canton of Switzerland.

A number of factors in the private lives of Chopin and Paderewski demonstrate that both had a definite penchant for luxury. The list of Chopin's addresses in Paris—Boulevard Poissonnière, Citè Bergère, Chaussé d'Antin, Rue Tronchet, Square d'Orléans, and Place Vendôme—reads like a Baedeker tour of the most fashionable quarters of Paris. Chopin's

apartments were invariably appointed with elegant furniture, drapery and artwork, while

Figure 25: A late nineteenth century photo of 5, Rue Tronchet, where Chopin lived in 1839. Polish Music Center Archives, USC.

94

his favorite Playel pianos—usually a grand and an upright—occupied a place of prominence in his salon. Smartly-tailored clothing, gloves and hats, and a live-in manservant completed the requirements of the comfortable life that Chopin had created for himself. Such luxury was possible because shortly after arriving in Paris Chopin became a sought-after teacher among the highest circles of society and earned handsome fees for his piano lessons.

For Paderewski, the world of comfort was at hand after his highly successful debut in Paris in 1888, followed by concerts in London and his first American tour. Always wanting a home of his own and finally able to afford one, Paderewski at first bought land and residences in Poland. Since he toured constantly, his properties were administered by various plenipotentiaries, an arrangement that in the long run proved difficult and costly. Kąśna Dolna, Paderewski's favorite Polish property in the south of Poland consisting of an early nineteenth century manor house and a substantial keep, was finally sold at a loss in 1903 after a great deal of enthusiastic investment. By that time, Paderewski already had acquired a palatial villa, Riond-Bosson near Lausanne, and lived there since 1899. It became the principal residence for Paderewski and his second wife, Helena. The house was run by a large staff and, whenever Paderewski was at home, there was a constant procession of guests and lavish dinner parties.

Just like Chopin, Paderewski was quite meticulous about his wardrobe and had the best tailors in London and Paris. Numerous photos taken throughout his life show him in smart attire, on and off the concert stage. Snapshots taken at Riond-Bosson during countless dinners and receptions prove that Paderewski was a genial and welcoming host with an aristocratic dignity and elegance about him. Young Artur Rubinstein visited Paderewski in Switzerland in the early 1900s and remembered how nervous he was after arriving at the cavernous and imposing residence:

I was really on the verge of running away, when—a miracle happened: the center door went wide open and there appeared the Sun—yes, the Sun. It was Paderewski, the still young Paderewski in his middle forties, dressed in a white suit, white shirt, and a while lavalière tie; a shock of golden hair, a mustache of the same color, and a little bush of hair between his mouth and his chin gave him the look of a lion. But it was his smile and his charm which made him appear so incredibly sunny.

He rushed up to me with short, quick steps, and with a few warm words of apology he put me instantly at ease and made me forget all my miseries. "I have heard nice things about you from Professor Joachim, whom I admire and respect," he said. "And I am also delighted that you are a Pole," he added, with a kind tap on my arm. "Now—play something you like to play."[1]

———————

When it came to social life, both Chopin and Paderewski were lionized by the highest aristocratic circles of Paris. Chopin's friendships with Princes Radziwiłł and Czartoryski, and the Rothschild family assured him with the entry to the *beau monde* of the capital. A refined individual and an intelligent musician with impeccable manners and excellent command of French, Chopin was a welcome guest at various dinners, receptions, soirees, and fêtes. Of course *le tout Paris musical* was present at Chopin's public concerts at Salons Pleyel on Rue Cadet in 1832 and in 1834 or at the Salle du Conservatoire; but even more coveted were the invitations to Chopin's private performances. Sometimes (and usually reluctantly) he invited his closest friends—Polish exiles but also fellow artists and musicians—to his apartment where he played for them. Liszt remembered one such meeting:

It was not without a struggle, without a repugnance slightly misanthropic, that Chopin could be induced to open his doors and piano, even to those whose friendship, as respectful as faithful, gave them a claim to urge such a request with eagerness. Without doubt more than one of us can still remember our first improvised evening with him, in spite of his refusal, when he lived at Chaussée d'Antin.[2]

Many Polish political émigrés travelled to Paris in a massive wave of emigration that followed the November 1830 Uprising in Poland. The most prominent—poets Adam Mickiewicz, Zygmunt Krasiński and Julian Niemcewicz among them—gravitated towards Prince Adam Czartoryski (1770-1861) and his Hôtel Lambert circle of Polish expatriates who were drawn together by their shared dream of bringing about Poland's independence. Aside from the obvious patriotic allegiances, Chopin's friendship with the Czartoryski family opened for him the most exclusive domains in the palatial quarters of Faubourg Saint-Germain or Faubourg Saint-Honoré. With standing invitations to the most refined circles of society, Chopin's professional and social success was guaranteed in every way. Prince Czartoryski's niece, Marcelina Czartoryska (1817-1894) was one of Chopin's best students and the closest of friends. Her piano playing was so accomplished that many considered her to be Chopin's true disciple. Princess Czartoryska and Chopin's sister, Ludwika, were at Chopin's deathbed. Countess Delfina Potocka (1807-1877) was another devoted friend of Chopin who was with him in his final days. Throughout his years in Paris, Chopin performed frequently for the Hôtel Lambert audiences of Polish exiles and top-ranking Parisian artists that included Chopin's cellist friend Franchomme and painter Delacroix, among others.

———————

Decades after Chopin's death, Poland was still a country partitioned and occupied by Russia, Prussia, and Austria. Following the pattern set during Chopin's days in Paris, political émigrés from Poland continued to be a strong presence in the French capital at the end of the nineteenth century, and many of them witnessed Paderewski's debut. Besides the Polish contingent, Paderewski's appearance at the Salle Érard in 1888 also attracted a number of prominent musicians. Tchaikovsky was there and so were two great orchestra conductors, Édouard Colonne (1838-1910) and Charles Lamoureux (1834-1899), as well as one of Chopin's celebrated pupils, Madame Camille Dubois (1830-1907). Just like Chopin in 1832, Paderewski in 1888 was the musical sensation of the season and he immediately received offers of concerts, both public and private. Conscious of the historical legacy of his great predecessor and already hailed in Poland by Dr. Tytus Chałubiński as "our second Chopin,"[3] Paderewski made his own pilgrimage to the addresses where Chopin had once resided.[4] Like Chopin, Paderewski courted the smartest set in town and became very close to a number of aristocratic ladies.

Paderewski's intimate friendship with Princess Rachel de Brancovan dates from the time of his Parisian debut. She was an able pianist and a pupil of Chopin's student, Madame Dubois. Princess Brancovan's salon was one of the most interesting in Paris and, as a result of this friendship, almost instantly Paderewski became a *de rigueur* guest at all kinds of elegant dinners and receptions. Anna, the twelve year old daughter of Princess de Brancovan, recorded this impression of Paderewski:

I saw a sort of archangel with red hair and blue eyes, pure, hard, searching and defiant, turned towards the soul. The strong florid neck was revealed by a collar folded down, from which flowed the tails of a foulard tie of sad white, the cloudy whiteness of fruit-blossom. His slender body betrayed its slimness in a black frock-coat of modest cloth which contrasted with the extreme pride in the face, outlined by a short mustache of gold, which also glowed on his strong chin … How I immediately loved that air of the vagabond of noble and proud race who seemed to have come slowly, day after day, from that Poland of kings, where everything that is marked with superiority arrogates to itself, with simplicity and bonhomie, the right to supreme self-respect!

It seemed to me that this strange young man, foreseeing our tenderness, had come to us along the roads of Podolia and Lithuania, wearing his elastic-sided *bottines* out in the hot dust or the cold winter that kills even the birds… Coiffed with light, his eyes attuned with the stars, a magus came to us; we loved him.[5]

With such an enthusiastic welcome into the best circles of Paris, Paderewski's career now could only advance at great speed.

———————

Chopin's presence and personal appearance were quite striking and truly distinguished—Berlioz once quipped to a friend that he ought to visit with Chopin, "for he is something which you have never seen—and someone you will never forget."[6] Chopin was slim and delicate, had beautiful hands and dressed with studied elegance, appearing more like an aristocratic gentleman than an artist. Still, he worked very hard and teaching was his main source of income. According to one estimate, Chopin taught well over one hundred students over the course of the last two decades of his life.[7] He rose early and gave lessons throughout the morning and well into the afternoon. A typical lesson cost about twenty francs and lasted about an hour, sometimes longer if the pupils were talented.[8] Chopin was always in demand as a teacher, much more so than Liszt or any other famous pianist living in Paris at that time. He was also a sought-after performer, but after the first few years in Paris he played in public only reluctantly. Chopin's infrequent public concerts were nonetheless very profitable—his last recital in Paris in February of 1848 was an instant sellout, with three hundred tickets going for twenty francs each.[9] Numerous aristocratic hosts in Paris and London vied for the privilege of hearing Chopin in an intimate setting, and salon concerts were another source of Chopin's income. For such appearances in England Chopin demanded an honorarium of twenty guineas.[10] When it came to selling his compositions to publishers—another important revenue stream—Chopin drove a very hard bargain and often engaged in long and detailed negotiations, causing publishers to engage in bidding wars. A glimpse into his dealings with Schlesinger and Pleyel in Paris and Probst & Wessel in Germany comes across quite forcefully in Chopin's letter from Marseilles to Julian Fontana, dated 17 March 1839:

> Thanks for all your trouble. Pleyel's a fool and Probst a rascal (he never gave me 1000 fr. for 3 manuscripts). No doubt you have received my long letter about Schlesinger; now I wish, and beg you, give my letter to Pleyel (who finds my manuscripts too dear). If I have to sell them cheap, I would rather let it be to Schlesinger than search for impossible new connections. As Schlesinger can always count on England, and as I am quits with Wessel, let him sell them to whom he likes. The same with the Polonaises in Germany; for Probst is a sly bird: I know him of old. Let Schlesinger sell to who he likes, not necessarily to Probst. It's nothing to me. He adores me, because he's skinning me. Only have clear understanding with him about the money, and don't give up the manuscripts except for cash. I will send Pleyel a *reconnaissance*. The fool, can't he trust either me or you? Good Lord, why must one have dealings with scoundrels! That Pleyel, who told me that Schlesinger was underpaying me, and now finds 500 fr. too much for a manuscript for all countries![11]

Having earned much, Chopin also spent significantly on apartments, furnishing, clothing, and—as the years went on and his health deteriorated—on various doctors and cures. Tragically, during the last year of his life Chopin had practically no income. He was too weak to teach or compose and, after returning from England, his finances were in desperate

Figure 26: Place Vendôme in a late nineteenth century photo. Chopin lived in the building on the right. Polish Music Center Archives, USC.

shape. He had no savings and no prospects for earning any income. Friends helped him pay for summer lodging in a spacious house at 74 Rue de Chaillot on the outskirts of Paris. In August of 1849 Chopin was overjoyed to welcome his sister Louise and her husband, who after much trouble and delay obtained a permit from the Russian authorities in Warsaw to travel to Paris. Afterwards, a magnificent anonymous gift of 25,000 francs from Chopin's student, Jane Stirling arrived just in time for Chopin to rent for the winter a beautiful apartment at 12, Place Vendôme, which was his last address in Paris.

———————

Just like Chopin, Paderewski was paid very well for his appearances and his honoraria were the envy of fellow musicians. Unlike Chopin however, during his lifetime Paderewski played thousands of concerts and earned a great fortune. Just his first American tour in 1891, for example, featured over one hundred concerts during a period of four and a half months, triumphant reviews, and a $100,000 profit.[12] Like Chopin before him, after his debut in Paris Paderewski was feted by high society in Paris and London. This honor also included invitations to perform "at home" in various salons and drawing rooms. Paderewski considered it a mixed blessing:

I had countless propositions to play in private houses in London, so many that it even became a difficulty to decide which to accept. I played in several places, but it was very hard, I found, because it was a form of entertainment that was not considered very seriously by the guests. [...] It was dreadful and I suffered agonies. I resented it to such a degree that on several occasions I was bold enough, and rude enough, to stop playing entirely and then apologize to those engaged in lively conversation for having interrupted them! At first I feared my sarcasm was too subtle for them but, after several experiences, it had its effect. [...]

In London at that time, a fee of sixty guineas was the highest price paid for an "at home." I am not speaking, of course, of Adelina Patti, who often sang privately. She always had a really tremendous fee. People would pay simply anything to get her. [...] Well, I played the first season for sixty guineas. Then I asked two hundred guineas after that, and for several years I received it. But as my concerts increased I was not in such need of earning extra money and could, therefore, dispense with the "at homes" and I was only too thankful to be able to refuse them. [...] So then I raised my price to five hundred guineas to make it practically impossible to engage me. That was unheard of and made a certain sensation, but gradually every artist raised his price so that rich people who had to entertain distinguished society, and who engaged great artists, had to pay very large sums for them, which was just and right.[13]

The salon concerts were also popular in America, and Paderewski played for numerous elite hosts all across the United States. During his 1907-1908 tour Paderewski performed at the White House for President Theodore Roosevelt:

During that tour I was invited to play at the White House, on which occasion I met President Theodore Roosevelt, who made a deep impression upon me. A strong, brilliant, and exceptionally well-informed man, knowing a great deal about European conditions, and particularly acquainted with my own country, which was chiefly due to his love of our remarkable writer, Sienkiewicz, who wrote those world-famous novels, *By Fire and Sword*, *Children of the Soil*, and *Quo Vadis*. He told me then that he traveled for years with Sienkiewicz's *Trilogy*.[14]

Paderewski played again at the White House on 20 January 1928 but his fondest memories were connected to private concerts he gave in Santa Barbara, California. After buying two ranches in 1914 in the nearby Paso Robles

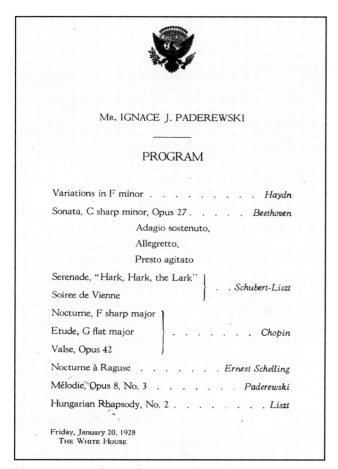

between San Francisco and Los Angeles and, among the houses he visited, he found his hosts in Santa Barbara especially welcoming:

> The most agreeable and enjoyable private house in which I played in America was that of Mrs. Bliss in Santa Barbara, and I played there a number of times. Whenever I was in California, she asked me to play for her and I always did it gladly, for her love and appreciation of music were very rare. To play in her house was an experience unlike anything else I found—it was like celebrating a Mass. The atmosphere of silence was like that of a temple. It was beautiful and inspiring.[15]

When it came to teaching, Paderewski—unlike Chopin—had only a handful of piano students during the course of his life. He taught briefly at the Music Institute in Warsaw after graduating from the school and in 1885 obtained a post at the Conservatoire in Strasbourg, where he remained for a year. Teaching, he found, was hard work:

> Yes, it seems I was a very good teacher, but I do not like it. I prefer to give ten concerts rather than one lesson! It takes much more of my energy, I assure you. It is a very exhausting profession.[16]

Among the select few, Zygmunt Stojowski (1870-1946) was Paderewski's most important student. Paderewski met the young Stojowski in Kraków in 1884 and from that time onwards became an older colleague and mentor to him.

on California's Central Coast, Paderewski rested between his tours and took cures in Paso's famous hot springs at least once a year. During his extended stays in California in the 1910s and the 1920s Paderewski visited many of his West Coast friends, scattered

Stojowski studied with Paderewski for a while in the early 1890s and immediately embarked on a successful solo career. In the early 1900s Stojowski moved to teach in New York and there fulfilled the role of Paderewski's occasional teaching assistant. Whenever young hopefuls approached Paderewski for piano lessons, he invariably referred them to Stojowski.[17] Besides Stojowski, in the 1890s Paderewski also taught Antonina Szumowska (a cousin of Paderewski's wife) who later married Paderewski's cellist friend, Józef Adamowski (1862-1930). During the last decade of his life Paderewski also consented to give summer master classes to a few young Polish pianists, including Aleksander Brachocki, Zygmunt Dygat, Stanisław Szpinalski, Henryk Sztompka, and Albert Tadlewski, with Witold Małcużyński also taking a few lessons with Paderewski in the mid-1930s.

Paderewski's legendary concert income matched his magnificent largesse. After selling properties in Poland, Paderewski settled down in Riond-Bosson, his splendid residence in Switzerland. He lived and entertained on a lavish scale but was also a most generous person who throughout his life championed countless causes. Stories of Paderewski's vast philanthropy abound—he tipped generously staffs of hotels, gave money for lessons to promising young musicians, bought thoughtful presents for friends, and so on. Still, much larger and more meaningful gestures were reserved for Paderewski's various civic and charitable initiatives in Europe and the United States. Among them were his donation of $4,300 to the Washington Arch Fund in 1892; the $10,000 "Paderewski Fund" for young American composers established in 1896; $28,500 raised in four concerts during December of 1925 for the American Legion; his legendary 1932 concert in Madison Square Garden that brought over $37,000 for the Musicians' Emergency Fund; as well as millions of dollars Paderewski raised through concertizing and speeches during the World War I years on behalf of Poland's independence. In Poland, America and Europe numerous public monuments were erected from Paderewski's funds; he helped establish newspapers, endow orphanages, and support a number of World War I veterans' associations. Such an extraordinary awareness of human needs, large and small, which he applied equally towards the single individual and whole societies, made Paderewski an unprecedented benefactor of mankind.

Although he earned vast sums of money, Paderewski also spent and gave away money on an epic scale. When Paderewski returned to the concert stage following his decade in politics and premiership of Poland after World War I, his comeback was motivated in part by the need to recover financially from his unprecedented charitable spree that had totaled several million dollars. In the last decade of his life, Paderewski's financial situation became gradually more precarious. After the death of his wife, Paderewski contemplated selling his house in Switzerland, as its upkeep proved very expensive. In his will drawn up in 1930 he stipulated that, in the event of his death, Riond-Bosson should be sold as soon as possible. There were at least two inquiries (in March of 1936 and January of 1937) from different buyers, but in the end his Swiss residence was not sold during Paderewski's lifetime.[18] Facing a serious financial shortfall, the only remaining option of generating the necessary income was for Paderewski to keep performing as long as possible and, with nothing short of a heroic determination, he pressed on as long as he could. The May 26, 1939 headline: "Paderewski Collapses in East Just Before Scheduled Concert" leads an article that ended as follows:

The huge Madison Square Garden audience filed out in stunned silence. When the pianist's illness was announced over the Garden's loudspeakers, many burst into tears. Some were still weeping as they left the auditorium. Some persons in the audience suggested that money refunded on tickets be left in the box office as a fund for Paderewski as a token of the affection and esteem of his admirers. A substantial number of ticket holders followed this suggestion. It appeared to be received with special enthusiasm because of the generally accepted rumor that Paderewski's tour was undertaken partly to meet a personal need of funds. Four other concerts remaining were cancelled.[19]

Paderewski returned to Switzerland a few months before the outbreak of World War II. He saw his beloved Poland invaded by Hitler's armies on September 1 and by the Soviets on September 17. His homeland once again was partitioned and his life's work in restoring Poland's independence now lay in ruins. In 1940 Paderewski watched with horror as France was overrun and quickly capitulated to the Nazis. Afterwards the neutrality of Switzerland looked very precarious and Paderewski decided to close his villa, pack whatever he could into two cars, and set out with his sister and a few members of his household on a journey to Portugal and then to America. Like thousands of refugees from Europe, Paderewski arrived in New York on 6 November 1940, his eightieth birthday.

It was a poignant anniversary and a telling coincidence: New York was the first American city Paderewski conquered in 1891 and the city where he died exactly fifty years later.

Figure 28: Maria Wodzińska: Frederic Chopin—a facsimile of the original watercolor from the collection of the National Museum in Warsaw, 1836. Collection of the Frederic Chopin Museum at the Frederic Chopin National Institute. Owned by the Frederic Chopin Society, F/6. Used by permission

Many interesting similarities emerge when a comparison of Chopin's and Paderewski's personal lives is made. For both artists their early love experiences remained unfulfilled. In Chopin's case, they were just youthful infatuations. Konstancja Gładkowska (1810-1889), a beautiful and accomplished singer, was Chopin's first emotional attachment. They met at concert in Warsaw in 1829 and remained friends until he left Poland a year later. Chopin often heard Gładkowska's performances and admired her musicianship but—besides a few rhetorical remarks in Chopin's letters and Konstancja's inscription in Chopin's diary—there is little evidence of a serious relationship. The final word from on this liaison came in a letter, written in December 1831 from Paris to Tytus Wojciechowski, when Chopin found out that Konstancja had married a banker in Warsaw:

Panna Gładkowska has married Grabowski, but that does not preclude platonic affections.[20]

Chopin's second love, Maria Wodzińska (1819-1896), came from a well-known aristocratic family in Warsaw. Her brothers attended school with Chopin and, since the Wodzińskis and the Chopins lived nearby, the two families often visited each other. When Chopin left Warsaw in 1830, Maria was only eleven; when he met her again in Dresden in September of 1835 she was sixteen and charming. After spending two weeks with Maria and her family, Chopin's departure caused a lot of regret and Maria wrote to him:

On Saturday, when you left us, we all went sadly, our eyes full of tears, around the parlor where a few minutes earlier you still belonged to our circle … My mother, in tears, reminded us time after time in some detail about the stay of her 'fourth son, Fryderyk…'[21]

Families on both sides seemed to encourage this romance and one of Maria's brothers, Antoni, who lived in Paris often called to visit Chopin. Later that fall, Chopin became seriously ill and the news of it was received with alarm by Maria's family, who visited with Chopin's parents in Warsaw. By the summer of 1836 however Chopin travelled to Marienbad to stay with the Wodzińskis and spent a delightful month of music-making, walks, and socializing with Maria and her family. He then followed them to Dresden, where his proposal was accepted on the condition that his health improves within a year. Taking a practical view of her daughter's future, Maria's mother asked a family doctor in Dresden for a consultation.

The medical opinion was that Chopin should avoid overexerting himself, shun late night dinners and receptions, and take care of his physical condition. After another health crisis during the following winter, the family recognized that Maria's marriage to a man suffering from recurring and possibly fatal illness was impractical. Madame Wodzińska's letters to Chopin became infrequent and Maria's postscripts to him noncommittal. During the summer of 1837 Chopin was still hoping for a rendezvous with Maria but as the invitation to join the Wodzińskis did not come, he travelled incognito to London for two weeks with his friend, Pleyel. Back in Paris Chopin resumed his heavy schedule of teaching, composing, performing at court and in public, and carrying on with his social life.

Although unlucky in love, Chopin had a few close and trusted friends upon whom he could always count in moments of need. Julian Fontana (1810-1869), a childhood companion from Warsaw, was a gifted pianist and Chopin's secretary in Paris for a number of years. It was Fontana who, after Chopin's death, fulfilled the request of his family to prepare for publication many of his friend's unpublished compositions. Tytus Wojciechowski (1808-1879) was another very close childhood friend to whom Chopin wrote many deeply personal letters. During the last months of his life Chopin was hoping to see Tytus, writing to him in Karlsbad on 20 August 1849:

> My Dearest One! It just needs for me to be as weak as this, and not able to move from Paris, when you are coming to Ostend. But I hope the Lord will allow you to come nearer to me. The doctors do not allow me to travel at all. I drink Pyrenean waters in my room, and your presence would do more for me than all physic. Yours till death, Fryderyk.[22]

Wojciechowski, who participated in the 1830 Uprising against Russia, was prevented by tsarist authorities from obtaining travel documents for Paris. Five weeks before he died, Chopin was still trying to arrange for his dear friend's visit:

> There has not been time enough to try for a permit for you to come here; I can't go to see to it myself, as I spend half the day in bed, so asked an influential friend to help me out. I shan't know anything for certain till Saturday. [...] It's my fault, for being ill; otherwise I would have met you somewhere in Belgium.
>
> Perhaps you will manage to get here. I am not selfish enough to demand that you should come here for me; I am so weak that you would have only a few hours of boredom and disappointment, alternating with a few hours of pleasure and good memories; and I should like the time that we spend together to be only a time of complete happiness. Yours always, Fryderyk.[23]

Count Wojciech Grzymała (1793-1871) was a Polish writer, political émigré and a father figure to Chopin in Paris. They saw each other frequently and corresponded very frequently until Chopin's death. The network of Chopin's friends was also augmented by a coterie of titled ladies in Paris, including Countess Delfina Potocka (a gifted singer and one of the most beautiful women in Europe), and Princess Marcelina Czartoryska, a formidable pianist, devoted student, and a staunch lifelong ally.

A few years later after their encounter, Maria Wodzińska married Count Józef Skarbek, the son of Fryderyk Skarbek on whose estate Chopin was born and after whom he was named. Maria's marriage ended in divorce eight years later. She then married Władysław Orpiszewski in 1848. After Chopin's death a packet of letters from the Wodzińskis was found among his papers. Inscribed *Moja bieda* [My grief] in Chopin's hand, it was a somber postscript to Chopin's hopes for happiness.

———————

Paderewski's family life began on a very tragic note. Having succeeded in obtaining his diploma in piano in 1878, Paderewski was offered a teaching position in Warsaw and tried to settle down:

> And now we come to a great event in my life. I think I shall have to say it very simply—I fell in love. I was only twenty at that time and in spite of the uncertainty of the future, I married. I wanted a home, a personal life of my own—a place and some one that belonged to me. I married in 1880 Antonina Korsak—a young girl who was a student at the Warsaw Conservatory. I had a little home of my own at last and I was happy—but it was a short happiness. A year later my wife died, leaving me alone with our child, a son. I had lived through a brief—a beautiful—experience. Even at twenty, one can plumb the heights and depths and feel the pain and mystery of life. I now faced another change—I must go forward alone. […] I realized very keenly that there was no future for me there in Warsaw except as a teacher, and so I determined to go to Berlin. I left my child with his grandmother, the mother of my wife, and went directly to Friedrich Kiel, a very famous teacher of that time, to study composition.[24]

It must have been very discouraging for Paderewski to balance his ambitions of becoming a serious musician and carry on as a twenty-one year old widower with a handicapped son.[25] Family situation notwithstanding, for the time being Paderewski decided to continue his musical education in Berlin and Vienna, and returned only occasionally to Poland to concertize and visit with his child. Strikingly handsome and bestowed with a magnetic personality, Paderewski always attracted a huge share of admirers; he always kept an active social life, attending concerts, receptions, dinner parties, and balls.

During his studies with Leschetizky in Vienna, Paderewski was on friendly terms with Annette Essipov (1851-1914), a young second wife of his piano teacher and a formidable pianist herself. Essipov's December 1888 concert at London's Crystal Palace shocked the usually reserved George Bernard Shaw, who wrote of Essipov's "terrible precision and unfailing nerve; her cold contempt for difficulties; her miraculous speed, free from any appearance of haste; her grace and finesse, without a touch of anything as weak as tenderness."[26] By special request, Paderewski's Piano Concerto was successfully premiered in Vienna by Annette Essipov under the baton of Hans Richter.

Besides perfecting his piano technique and composing, Paderewski's days in Vienna were also graced by his friendships with distinguished members of Polish aristocracy, including Countess Angèle Potocka and Prince Czartoryski.[27] Just like Chopin, who was fondly remembered by all his childhood friends for the fun and games that his presence always seemed to provoke, Countess Potocka had a similarly warm remembrance of young Paderewski's days in Vienna:

He was what might almost be called a genius for devising impromptu amusements, and when a number of young people were assembled in the house, he and Annette Essipov were always the life of the party, entering into the spirit of the games with childish enjoyment.[28]

Like Chopin after his debut in Paris, Paderewski's phenomenal success in the French capital in 1888 not only assured his rapid ascent in the world of music but also opened doors to the glittering set of Parisian aristocracy for him. Madame Essipov herself introduced Paderewski to Princess Rachel de Brancovan, a young widow with two children. She was a talented pianist who studied with Madame Dubois, a student of Chopin. By 1890 Paderewski was intimate with Princess Brancovan, spending time with her in Paris, vacationing in her Swiss villa on Lake Geneva, and also visiting with her various fashionable European resorts. During that time Paderewski toured Europe and the United States, worked on a number of compositions, including the *Polish Fantasia* for piano and orchestra, and sketched out his opera *Manru*. His relationship with Princess Brancovan lasted until 1896 and the fact that he settled in Switzerland is also partially due to her influence. It was she who pointed out to Paderewski that a large residence near Lausanne was advertised for rental. With three extremely successful American tours behind him, Paderewski had ample means to afford the rental of Riond-Bosson, a splendid villa in the vicinity of Princess Brancovan's own chateau. Paderewski's new abode was located above the shores of Lake Geneva and had an impressive view of Mont Blanc. Paderewski and his chronically ill son, Alfred, liked the house immediately, and Paderewski negotiated the lease at once.[29] After a year Paderewski bought Riond-Bosson outright. The house—sometimes referred to as a "chateau"—was surrounded by about one hundred acres of parkland, orchards, and vineyards, which was much to Paderewski's liking. He had finally arrived on the world scene as a preeminent pianist and composer, and now also had a residence worthy of his artistic and social standing. Making Riond-Bosson into a proper family seat would be the next step.

———

Figure 29: Ludwik Wawrynkiewicz: George Sand—a copy of the fragment of the double portrait of George Sand and Frederic Chopin by Eugène Delacroix (1838) in the collection of the Ordrupgaard Museum in Copenhagen [1979]. Collection of the Frederic Chopin Museum at the Frederic Chopin National Institute. Owned by the Frederic Chopin Society, M/1727. Used by permission

After about seven years of bachelorhood in Paris, Chopin decided to cast his lot in 1838 with a French writer, George Sand (1804-1876), a divorced mother with two children.[30] Six years older than Chopin, Sand was well-known for her copious literary output and the number of lovers she had before and after separating in 1835 from her husband, Baron François Casimir Dudevant (1795-1871). Chopin first met George Sand in October of 1836 at a party given by Franz Liszt and his mistress, Countess Marie d'Agoult. Their apartment on Rue Lafitte was not far from Chopin's flat on Chaussée d'Antin.[31] Sand, whose novels were often based on assorted details of her private life, had several very public affairs, most notably with Prosper Mérimée and Alfred de Musset. Before meeting Chopin, Sand was already among the circle of Chopin's friends: besides Liszt and Countess Marie d'Agoult, Sand knew poet Adam Mickiewicz and publisher Aleksander Jełowicki (1804-1877) fairly well. By October 1837 Sand was helping Count Wojciech Grzymała, another close friend of Chopin, in organizing a bazaar sale for impoverished Polish refugees.[32] Also among Sand's friends were the Spanish Consul in Paris, Manuel

Marliani and his wife, Charlotte, who in April 1838 gave a party to which Chopin, Grzymała, and few other Polish acquaintances of the hosts were invited.[33] It was after that dinner that Sand dispatched a note to Chopin, *On vous adore—George*, which Chopin kept to the end of his days. In spite of the fact that at that time she had a lover, a novelist and playwright Jean Pierre Félicien Mallefille, George Sand wrote a long letter to Grzymała in May 1838, asking him for advice regarding the possibility of a relationship with Chopin. By June George Sand was back in Paris and her liaison with Chopin had begun. When Mallefille (who wrote gushing reviews of Chopin's music) discovered that he was being replaced, an ugly and public row broke out with an attempted assault on Sand by her jilted lover and a threat of a duel between him and Chopin. Given the circumstances, Sand decided to travel with her children to Mallorca for the winter season and departed from Paris in the middle of October. After his usual prevaricating, Chopin finally made up his mind to forgo a season of teaching and concerts in Paris and left for the south of France at the end of the month, where he joined Sand and her family. In early November they landed in Mallorca. In his 19 November 1838 letter to Julian Fontana (who was left to deal with Chopin's apartment and his business affairs) Chopin was ecstatic:

I am in Palma, among palms, cedars, cacti, olives, pomegranates, etc. Everything the Jardin des Plantes has in its greenhouses. A sky like turquoise, a sea like lapis lazuli, mountains like emerald, air like heaven. Sun all day, and hot; everyone in summer clothing; at night guitars and singing for hours. Huge balconies with grapevines overhead; Moorish walls. Everything looks towards Africa, as the town does. In short, glorious life! […] I shall probably lodge in a wonderful monastery, the most beautiful situation in the world; sea, mountains, palms, a cemetery, a Crusaders' church, ruined mosques, aged trees, thousand-year old olives. Ah, my dear, I am coming alive a little—I am near to what is most beautiful. I am better …[34]

But the idyll in Mallorca's exotic surroundings soon ended. The weather turned cold and rainy and Chopin began to cough blood. Worse was still to come: the owners of the house in Palma where he stayed feared contagion and asked the vacationers to find new accommodations. On 28 December Chopin reported to Fontana that they moved out of Palma to:

[…] Valdemosa, a few miles away. It's a huge Carthusian monastery, stuck down between rocks and sea, where you may imagine me, without white gloves or hair curling, as pale as ever, in a cell with such doors as Paris never had for gates. The cell is the shape of a tall coffin, with an enormous dusty vaulting, a small window, outside the window orange trees, palms and cypresses, opposite the window my bed on rollers, under a Moorish filigree rosette. Besides the bed is a square *claque nitouchable* for writing, which I can scarcely use, and on it (a great *luxe* here) a leaden candlestick with a candle. Bach, my scrawls and (not my) waste paper—silence—you could scream—there would still be silence. Indeed, I write to you from a strange place. […] Nature is benevolent here, but the people are thieves, because they never see strangers, and so don't know how much to demand. Oranges can be had for nothing, but a trouser button costs a fabulous sum. But all that is just a grain of sand, when one has this sky, this poetry that everything breathes here, this coloring of the most exquisite places, color not yet faded by man's eyes. No one has yet scared away the eagles that soar every day above our heads![35]

Other problems included the lack of a suitable piano for Chopin and the delay caused by the Palma Customs Office in releasing the instrument sent to him from Paris by Pleyel. The weather continued to be unpredictable and Chopin was mostly confined to the monastery. By mid-February Chopin and Sand were tired of their Mallorcan adventures and returned to France. They spent several weeks in Marseilles, recuperating after the ordeal of the miserable vacations capped by the stormy sea crossing on their return to the mainland. Before returning to Paris, the couple passed the summer months of 1839 in Nohant, Sand's ancestral home in central France, where Chopin finally regained his health. With the coming of the fall, Chopin and Sand moved back to Paris—in late September Chopin instructed Fontana to rent an apartment on Rue Tronchet,[36] while Sand moved to Rue Pigalle about a mile away. The year 1840 was the only summer that both Chopin and Sand spent in Paris. Otherwise, for the first time in his life, Chopin's schedule became routine for the next several years. After spending fall and winter in Paris, by late spring he and Sand would move to Nohant for long summer sojourns. With such an arrangement in place, Chopin could concentrate on teaching whilst in Paris and devote his time to composing during his holidays in the country.

Sand, who throughout her life was a prolific writer and kept up her literary career amidst a stormy personal life, made a valiant effort to take care of Chopin and provide him with as much comfort as possible. She had played a maternal role vis-à-vis almost every one of her lovers, who—like Chopin—were invariably much younger and often in poor health. After Chopin's death, Sand was more critical of their relationship in her memoirs, claiming that she "drifted into a liaison which lasted several years" and felt "alarmed at the task."[37]

Although Sand's affections for Chopin may have become less intense with the passage of years and with Chopin's worsening health, he was really dependent on her for organizing his life and looking after his welfare. Chopin wrote tenderly of Sand when she was unwell and appreciated how she cared for him in Mallorca.[38] When Chopin heard that his friend Grzymała was ill, he wrote him from Marseilles on 12 April 1839:

> You know, you would love her even more if you knew her as I know her today … How I would look after you! I have been taught how to look after people! And you would enjoy being looked after by me, for you know my feeling towards you. I have never been of any use to you, but perhaps I should be able to nurse you now.[39]

Sand's reverence for Chopin's music was also an important factor in their relationship. Chopin always needed someone close to him who understood and supported his music and Sand was able to provide this for him: in Paris he was left to work undisturbed with his students and during the summers he had the sunniest room and a piano in Nohant, where he wrote many of his most enduring masterpieces.

In 1842 Sand and Chopin moved to Square d'Orléans—a private enclave of elegant buildings facing a small central garden. Their apartments were on the opposite side of the courtyard; Sand lived at No. 5, Chopin at No. 9. This allowed Chopin and Sand to be together or separate and receive company or work on their own projects undisturbed. The Square was something of an artists' colony with neighbors like composers Charles Gounod and Charles-Valentin Alkan, singer Pauline Viardot and her husband Louis, and writer Alexandre Dumas *père*. The first half of the 1840s was probably the happiest time for Chopin—he performed at Salle Pleyel in 1841 and 1842 to great acclaim and had an established domestic life with a devoted companion as well as a host of old friends who were just as close and faithful.

When Chopin's father died in 1844, Chopin's sister Ludwika came to Paris with her husband and George Sand immediately offered Ludwika keys to her apartment. Chopin and his family also travelled to Nohant in late summer on Sand's invitation. Afterwards, in Chopin's letters to his sister, he referred to George Sand as "the Lady of the House" and there is no reason to presume that Ludwika saw the hostess as anything more than a caring and close friend of her younger brother.

Unfortunately, from about this point onwards the relations between Chopin and Sand began to deteriorate. The break—when it finally came three years later—was mainly caused by Sand's children. Her son, Maurice, resented Chopin from the moment he was "added" as a new family member on the escapade to Mallorca. Sand's daughter, Solange, who tried to study piano, was always much friendlier towards Chopin. During their vacations in Mallorca, Sand's children were still quite young, but by the mid-1840s they had entered adulthood. Maurice's growing dislike of Chopin and his presence in the life of his mother was augmented by Solange's manipulative and impetuous nature. When Maurice instigated several violent arguments with Chopin and Sand sided with her son, the die was cast upon the future of their relationship. In the meantime, Solange was engaged to a well-bred young country gentleman, but eloped with Auguste Jean Baptiste Clésinger, an ex-soldier and an ambitious sculptor, instead. As this drama unfolded, Sand kept Chopin in the dark about her family's affairs and Solange's future. When Solange caused a huge row after arriving at Nohant with her newly-minted husband (leading to fisticuffs between Maurice, Sand, and Clésinger) and was thrown out of the house, she wrote a completely false account of the event to Chopin, asking him for help. Not knowing what had transpired, he agreed to lend her his carriage and wrote about it to Sand. Furious that Chopin was taking the side of her daughter, Sand wrote a letter that was described by Chopin's friend, Delacroix as "inhuman." Her final words were:

> [...] I shall not suffer from this bizarre betrayal. Farewell, my friend! May you be healed quickly of your ailments, and I hope for it now (I have my reasons for that), and I shall thank God for this bizarre dénouement of nine years of exclusive friendship. Give me your news occasionally. It is useless ever to return to the rest.[40]

Meanwhile, Solange was back in Paris and, at least for a time, Chopin believed her side of the story. When he finally replied to Sand, there was no doubt that the relationship was over.

Yet another aspect of the fallout was contributed by Sand in the form of her novel, *Lucrezia Floriani*. It was published in installments in *Le Courier français*, beginning in the summer of 1846. Sand, who throughout her literary career was practically incapable of inventing a fictional plot, chose this time the subject of a breakup between long-time lovers. Her book was a very thinly disguised *roman à clé* where the character of chronically ill Eastern European Prince, Karol de Rosewald,

Figure 30: Chopin's salon at Place Vendôme. After a watercolour by Kwiatkowski. Reproduced in H. Opieński, *Chopin*. Polish Music Center Archives, USC

is an unflattering portrait of Chopin in all but a name. The demanding Prince lives with a middle-aged actress, Lucrezia, who sacrifices her life and career to care for and satisfy the needs of her companion. In case any reader was still in doubt about this charade, the second edition of *Lucrezia Floriani* that came out after Chopin's death was illustrated by Sand's son Maurice, and his drawings of Prince Karol look very much like Chopin's portrait. With his reserved and private nature, Chopin must have been deeply disappointed by such public airing of details from his private life. He was too refined to comment on the gossip that followed the publication of Sand's novel, but finally admitted in a moment of weakness during his trip to England in November of 1848:

Never have I cursed anyone, but everything now is so unbearable that I think I should feel easier if I could curse *Lucrezia*.[41]

After spending nine years together, Chopin and Sand parted ways in 1847. They saw each other again only once, on 4 March 1848, outside a friend's apartment. Chopin informed Sand about the birth of Solange's daughter, she politely inquired about his health. Chopin then asked a porter to open the door and walked out of the building. This terse exchange sealed the history of their lives together.

Later that year Chopin embarked on his second visit to England. He was invited there by his student, Jane Stirling. His health was already very precarious and getting worse. In spite of considerable difficulties, he spent several months in England, then in Scotland, visiting with Jane's family and friends and performing in a few private and public concerts. He returned to Paris in late

Figure 31: Paderewski and his wife, Helena, shortly after their marriage. Polish Music Center Archives, Zygmunt and Luisa Stojowski Collection.

November, exhausted and ill. He was too weak to compose or teach and received only his closest friends. His financial situation was very difficult; only thanks to a very generous gift from Jane Stirling Chopin was able to spend his last months in comfortable lodgings. Less than a year after returning from London he died in Paris at the age of thirty-nine.

After a tragic beginning to his married life, Paderewski decided to remarry twenty years later, when he was almost forty. His bride was someone who had been close to his heart for many years and—most importantly—she was the one who greatly helped his career by partially assuming the responsibilities of caring for Paderewski's ailing son. Her name was Helena, Baroness von Rosen-Górska and, just like Chopin's partner George Sand, she was of noble birth, a few years older, married, and had a child. Paderewski met her after completing his studies in Warsaw. Helena's husband, Władysław Górski, a violinist and composer, was a professor in Warsaw and later a soloist and member of the Lamoureux Orchestra in Paris, where he also taught a chamber music course.[42] The Górskis had a music salon in Warsaw which Paderewski often attended and where he also performed solo or in a duet with Helena's husband. Górski and Paderewski often concertized together, first in Poland and later in Paris. The Górskis were also present at Paderewski's Parisian debut. Paderewski's second concert in Paris was a chamber music program where Górski performed Paderewski's Sonata for Violin and Piano with the composer. Władysław and Helena Górski continued their tradition of hosting a music salon at their apartment on Rue Boissière on Fridays and Paderewski came as often as he could.[43] Another reason for their close friendship was that Paderewski's ailing son, Alfred, was brought from Poland to Paris, where he was cared for by Helena. This arrangement appealed to Paderewski when he was on tour; he knew he did not need to worry about Alfred, who by that time had become Helena's de facto ward. Helena on the other hand, was attracted to Paderewski from the start and fascinated by this talented young man whose life took such a tragic turn. But as a married woman she held back, and with Alfred around her house she knew Paderewski would never be far away. During the first decade of his friendship with Helena, Paderewski was still studying, first in Berlin then in Vienna. By the time Paderewski and the Górskis settled in Paris in the late 1880s, there was a long history of friendship between the three of them.

Helena's father, Baron von Rosen, came from the Baltic provinces of Poland and served in the Tsarist army. Wounded in the Crimean War, he was recuperating on the island of Corfu, where he fell in love and married a Greek woman. She died in childbirth and left him with a daughter, Helena, who inherited her mother's beauty. Thus, as far as their marriages were concerned, the fate of Helena's father and that of Paderewski was nearly identical—a fact that in due course drew Helena closer to her beloved pianist. The Górskis had a son, Wacław (affectionately known as Wacio) and raised Alfred Paderewski as their second son, alongside Wacio.

The early 1890s were a tumultuous time for Paderewski. His career was on a meteoric rise with concerts in Europe and tours of America where he earned fabulous sums; yet he still occasionally performed with Górski and visited his son and Helena regularly. He was also in great demand as a bachelor at countless social engagements all across Paris and carried on a number of liaisons, most conspicuously with Princess de Brancovan who—incredibly—was a close friend of Helena Górska. Throughout this, Helena (much like George Sand) tried to be Paderewski's mother, pouring out her heart in letters to him:

You have left, dear child, and once again all is emptiness and sadness. I want to thank you with all my heart for the moments of happiness you gave me, those moments of consolation and respite which you brought me … You were not only a lover to me but also the best of friends, who drew me back with chivalry from the abyss over which I stood.[44]

In another note, she was dispensing advice on musical and financial matters:

Look after and care for those darling paws … Live for the present, my child—do not look at the future.[45]

When Paderewski was touring the United States, Helena became deeply unhappy. She felt lonely, saw her marriage failing, and was terribly afraid that with Paderewski's growing fame she might become just a forgotten episode from his earlier days. She bombarded Paderewski with letters, demanding news and proof of his unfaltering devotion. She asked if Paderewski could find a job for Górski in America, because he irritated her terribly and she wanted him to be far away.[46] She also added:

While little Alfred needs me, I shall stay with him—and afterwards I shall disappear, and will not be a burden to anyone, not even to you, my darling one.[47]

By that time, Helena's husband realized what was going on between Paderewski and his wife and agreed in 1895 to seek an annulment from the Catholic Church. When it was granted a few years later—on the grounds that when Helena married at the age of eighteen, her father had given only written consent—Helena and Paderewski could finally be married. They did so in Warsaw on 31 May 1899 and spent part of their honeymoon at Paderewski's estate, Kąśna Dolna, in southern Poland. Afterwards they travelled to Paderewski's villa in Switzerland. Paderewski's son, Alfred, loved the beautiful lakeshore near Lausanne, and so, right at the beginning of the twentieth century Paderewski's family life became once more stabilized. Helena and Alfred enjoyed the spectacular comforts of Riond-Bosson and its huge park, while Paderewski continued pursuing his career.

Unfortunately, a tragedy soon followed. Alfred Paderewski died of pneumonia in 1901 and was buried in Paris. Afterwards, life at Riond-Bosson became a cycle of Paderewski's worldwide touring, sojourns at home when he practiced for his concerts and devoted time to composition, and entertaining friends—musicians, artists, aristocrats, politicians, and numerous Polish compatriots—at sumptuous dinner parties. Helena Paderewska indulged in her hobby of raising poultry and educating poor young women from Poland. To take his mind off music, Paderewski pursued gardening and viticulture. Riond-Bosson became an experimental site for testing the newest methods in grape and fruit tree cultivation; at the same time the imposing aviary where Madame Paderewska reigned supreme became a breeding ground for her prizewinning chickens.[48] Paderewski's older sister, Antonina, who was recently widowed, came to Switzerland and, for the next four decades became *de facto* majordomo at the house.

The next big development in Paderewski's domestic life was the acquisition of extensive land properties in California. As a result of touring America, Paderewski became very fond of the country, its system of government, and its people:

Nowhere in the world could one observe such a strong influence of the environments upon the intellectual and emotional moulding of the individual as here, in this wonderful country of yours. People of various races, languages and creeds, people born in the countries where a narrow and selfish nationalism has been prevailing as an almost religious dogma, after having been brought up here, or even after having spent a number of years in this atmosphere of freedom, of equal opportunities of that large and broad equity which the English language calls "fair play," acquire in a degree American mentality, American fellow feeling. They become apt to understand that other people may also have rights to enjoy that freedom, that equality of opportunities and that fair play.[49]

The immediate reason for Paderewski's land purchases in Paso Robles on California's Central Coast was the recurrence of inflammation in his hand tendons and muscles. He was advised to visit hot springs in Paso Robles and take a cure there. He fell under the spell of this quaint town and its gently rolling hills with groves of majestic oak trees. He also fell under a spell of a local real estate promoter:

It was in February, 1914, that I bought my ranch in Paso Robles. There were two reasons for buying that large property, which has since been a cause of much trouble and expense. First of all, I was under a feeling of great gratitude to the place itself for my recovery, and secondly, I was pursued constantly, and I may say, almost violently, by the physician of the establishment who had a decided passion for the real-estate business, and I was completely at his mercy! He used to come to me and preach about acquiring land there because it was so profitable, such an opportunity for investment for the future. He was as deeply interested in that as he was in his patients, apparently. It had its amusing side, of course, because I was helpless—at his mercy. His attacks upon me took place when I was in the baths—in mud up to my neck! I could not protest, I could not resist, and he never let up. I was in a trap. I must add in justice, however, I was probably quite a willing victim, for I really loved the place and was grateful besides. […]

I developed the place greatly. I planted many hundreds of acres of almond trees, prune trees, walnut trees and even a vineyard, which for a time had great success because of the Swiss-Italian colonists who live not far away, and bought the grapes to make their own wine. But it is expensive to keep up. I have there a very good man, who was practically educated at my expense because he made his apprenticeship in Switzerland. For a time my garden here at Riond-Bosson in Morges has been considered as a model orchard in the whole of the Swiss Confederation. Yes, I loved Paso Robles before and after I bought it. It proved to be another gold mine, as I have already said, a mine that you pour gold into but never take any out! There have been many such gold mines in my life.[50]

Figure 32: Paderewski speaking in June 1915. His political appearances during World War I were very effective, as he passionately stated his arguments for Poland's independence. The Paso Robles Collection, Polish Music Center, USC. All rights reserved

119

Figure 33: Paderewski with Zygmunt Stojowski and "Daddy" Hemphill, Paderewski's ranch administrator in Paso Robles. The Paso Robles Collection, Polish Music Center, USC.

Paderewski spent the years of World War I travelling across America, speaking to huge crowds and advocating the restoration of Poland's independence. His efforts reached the highest levels of the U.S. government, including President Wilson, and were phenomenally successful. Thanks to Paderewski, President Wilson's famous "Fourteen Points" speech made to the Congress in January 1918 included a provision for the creation of an independent Poland with access to the sea.[51] Paderewski later became Poland's first head of state and also a delegate to the Peace Conference in Versailles and to the League of Nations.

Meanwhile, his investment in ranches in Paso Robles where he planted almond trees and cultivated Zinfandel and Petit Syrah grapes was probably intended as a retirement income project. But before retirement plans would become a reality, Paderewski decided to return to his concert career after a decade spent in politics, and also came back to live in Switzerland after a long absence from his villa during the war years. After resuming in 1922 his American tours, which continued to be his main source of income, Paderewski came to Paso Robles on an annual basis, resting, taking cures, and supervising the management of his ranches. Throughout the twenty-five years he owned his California ranches, Paderewski's imprint on local agriculture was significant—having initiated large-scale wine production on California's Central Coast, he would undoubtedly be proud to see how it thrives today. Paderewski's wines were judged to be among the ten best in California by the *Los Angeles Times* in the mid-1930s. He was the celebrity resident of Paso Robles and the entire town welcomed him with pomp and circumstance every time he came to stay.[52] Helena Paderewska had her own ranch, Rancho Santa Helena, where she could experiment with plantings of fruit trees, grapes, and ornamental flowers and shrubs.

Throughout the rest of the 1920s, Paderewski's life fell into a routine—from his base in Switzerland he concertized around Europe during the summer and early fall and then embarked on his American tours. Always travelling in his private Pullman car, he began his concerts on the East Coast in late fall and then moved through the South. By early spring Paderewski was on the West Coast, breaking his performing schedule by resting in Paso Robles for a few weeks. Afterwards he returned to New York via the upper Midwest and, by May, sailed for Europe, usually on the French Line.

During the late 1920s Helena Paderewska's health began to deteriorate. After developing progressive dementia, she could not accompany her husband on the road and was cared for at Riond-Bosson by her personal secretary and companion, Helena Liibke. Helena Paderewska died on 16 January 1934 and was buried in Paris next to Alfred Paderewski. Her death was a milestone in Paderewski's life and Paderewski—just like Chopin—spent his last years without a longtime companion.

The happy era of entertaining at Riond-Bosson was largely over and Paderewski, realizing that its upkeep was a serious drain on his resources, seriously considered selling the property in the late 1930s. His legendary stamina gradually fading, he appeared in concert only reluctantly, but made a few radio broadcasts and played a leading role in the film *Moonlight Sonata* directed by Lothar Mendes. His twentieth—and last—tour of the United States took place in 1939. Paderewski's final concert in New York had to be cancelled—he was simply too tired to go on. He returned to Riond-Bosson on the eve of World War II but a peaceful retirement was not in the cards. A year after the war engulfed most of Europe Paderewski had to flee in September of 1940, fearing that Hitler might also try to invade Switzerland. When, after a long and harrowing trip across war-torn Europe he reached the coast of Portugal and boarded a ship for America, Paderewski became one of countless refugees from the rapidly escalating world conflict. He arrived in New York on 6 November 1940, his eightieth birthday, and spent the remaining seven months of his life lobbying the U.S. government and the public to "fight Hitler before he masters the Atlantic."[53] Paderewski died in New York on 29 June 1941.

———————

A juxtaposition of the character and temperament of these two great artists reveals some interesting differences. Chopin was a rather private person who preferred a company of close friends and was happy to move only within fairly intimate circles. Towards those he trusted and knew a long time he could be witty, warm, and full of good cheer and passion for living. Dressed impeccably, cultured and urbane in his speech, for strangers Chopin remained on guard, reserved and distant. French pianist Antoine-François Marmontel recalled that:

> Chopin was surrounded, adulated and protected by a mall entourage of enthusiastic friends who defended him from unwelcome visitors or second rate admirers. Access to him was difficult; as he himself told his pianist and composer friend Stephen Heller, one had to make several attempts before one could succeed in meeting him.[54]

Chopin's preference for self-enforced solitude was articulated in a Christmas Day 1831 letter from Paris to his trusted friend, Tytus Wojciechowski:

> You know how easily I make acquaintances; how I like to gossip with people about banalities—well, I have no end of such acquaintance; and not one with whom I can be sad. [...] You would not believe how I long for a pause, to have no one come near me all day long. When I am writing to you, I cannot bear to hear the doorbell... [...] I am gay on the outside, especially among my own folk (I count Poles my own); but inside something gnaws at me; some presentiment, anxiety, dreams—or sleeplessness—melancholy, indifference—desire for life, and the next instant, desire for death: some kind of sweet peace, some kind of numbness, absent-mindedness; and sometimes definite memories worry me.[55]

Paderewski, on the other hand, was an individual who throughout his life retained a strong and clear sense of mission; his quest to succeed in music was truly unparalleled in its relentless drive and resolve. Whereas Chopin's genius was natural and effusive in the way it revealed itself to the public, Paderewski simply had to work very hard throughout his life to reach a similar depth of communicating with his public. Chopin's success came easily and quickly; Paderewski's road to success was long and winding. Once he attained his goals, Paderewski quickly realized that he was in position help others. After his third American tour, he wrote to Mr. Steinway in April of 1896:

> The generous support I have found in this country enables me to accomplish one of my most ardent wishes. I do not intend to thank the American people for all they have done for me, because my gratitude to your noble nation is, and will be, beyond expression. But I desire to extend a friendly hand toward my American brother musicians, toward those, who, less fortunate than myself, are struggling for recognition or encouragement. To this purpose I send you herewith $10,000, asking you to accept, together with Col. H. L. Higginson, of Boston, and Dr. William Mason, of New

York, the trusteeship of this sum. […] I take no pride in making this endowment. The amount is a modest one, and my personality, in spite of all the success, is of little importance. I only hope that it will prove to be useful, and that your younger composers will not consider as a gift, but as a debt, this little encouragement coming from one who found in their land all happiness to which an artist can aspire.[56]

Unlike the intensely private and guardedly reserved Chopin, throughout his life Paderewski repeatedly demonstrated his unprecedented generosity to all kinds of causes. Paderewski clearly was an optimist and a dreamer, who believed in a positive attitude towards life, and whose caring spirit for others was well-known and universally admired. His energy, noble bearing and electrifying presence were strongly felt by his concert audiences, by those he met in private, and by the multitudes he addressed as a successful politician.

When it came to appreciating art, both Chopin and Paderewski were discriminating connoisseurs whose rather conservative tastes were clearly reflected in the arrangement of their private spaces. Both men enjoyed visiting museums and various architectural sites. Chopin expressed his admiration of the galleries in Dresden and deeply enjoyed his visit in Vienna's Cathedral during Christmas of 1830:

… I strode along slowly alone, and at midnight went into St. Stephens's. When I entered there was no one there. Not to hear the mass, but just to look at the huge building at that hour, I got into the darkest corner at the foot of a Gothic pillar. I can't describe the greatness, the magnificence of those huge arches. It was quiet; now and then the footsteps of a sacristan lighting candles at the back of the sanctuary, would break in on my lethargy. A coffin behind me, a coffin under me; only the coffin above me was lacking. A mournful harmony all around—I never felt loneliness so clearly.[57]

When he settled in Paris, Chopin carefully decorated his rooms with antique furnishings, exquisite wallpaper and elegant draperies, personally selecting colors and fabrics even if his friends were charged with purchasing and putting everything in place. Chopin was also very particular in selecting the addresses for his residences—he had lists of favorite streets and

Figure 34: Paderewski's villa in Switzerland. The Paso Robles Collection, Polish Music Center, USC.

123

precise requirements for the kinds of spaces he would find acceptable.

Young Paderewski too was fond of visiting museums and various art exhibits, especially when he studied in Vienna—he reported his impressions in several letters to Helena Górska many years before she finally became his wife. In May 1886 Paderewski's friend and music director at the Strasbourg Cathedral persuaded him to travel to Basel and hear a concert. Paderewski also did a little sightseeing and related his impressions to Helena:

> […] Yesterday at the cathedral they gave the *Missa solemnis* Beethoven—the whale of music. I went—for 25 borrowed marks, true—but had as much fun as if for 26 of my own. A pretty little city, the location and the banks of the Rhine are gorgeous, the cathedral magnificent, the museum interesting, the music decent. I have not heard such superb acoustics. In the performance, there were many errors, tempi often inappropriate; the soloists, with the exception of the soprano, were shabby and shabbiest of all was the violinist; even so, the work itself, for the third time already, made a powerful impression on me. I also had a pleasant experience at the Museum. There is a very numerous and interesting collection of Holbein, a few things by Dürer, there is also Ruisdael, Brueghel, Teniers as well as a few of the 'baser' Italians, but that all did not take me as much time as five paintings by Boecklin. What a hell of an imagination, what an original color scheme, and what wealth of technique!! Looking at the *Battle of the Centaurs*, I got hit in the face with shock and, as a humble Christian, I turned the other cheek to the landscapes.[58]

After buying Riond-Bosson, a large and rambling Art Nouveau style property on the shores of Lake Geneva, Paderewski transformed the interior into a fascinating mélange of styles, colors and textures. The magnificent entry hall with its huge staircase was reminiscent of an operatic set. Potted palms, large Chinese vases, heavy curtains and rugs added

Figures 35-36: The salon at Riond-Bosson with Paderewski at his Steinway grand (top), and his small practice studio upstairs. The Paso Robles Collection, Polish Music Center, USC. All rights reserved

to the sense of opulence and drama. Two Steinway grand pianos had the pride of place in the salon; covered with heavy silk drapes the instruments also served to display the numerous portraits and autographed photos of popes, kings, heads of state, musicians, military leaders, and other important world personalities who were Paderewski's close friends. There was also a collection of paintings all around the house, including the portrait of Helena by Henryk Siemiradzki (1843-1902), as well as portraits of Paderewski by his friends, Edward Burne-Jones (1833-1898) and Lawrence Alma-Tadema (1836-1912). A famous triptych by Jacek Malczewski (1854-1929) was prominently displayed along the entire wall of the dining room.[59]

Literature was another common denominator between Chopin and Paderewski. Both were well-read and throughout their lives remained on friendly terms with several literary figures. For most of his adult life Chopin was surrounded by distinguished poets and leading figures in the literary set, most notably Adam Mickiewicz, Stefan Witwicki (1801-1847), Heinrich Heine (1797-1856) and, of course, George Sand. The influence of Mickiewicz's epic poetry expressed itself indirectly in Chopin's Ballades; in addition

Figure 37: A view of the salon at Riond-Bosson. The Paso Robles Collection, Polish Music Center, USC.

Chopin also set two of Mickiewicz's poems to music. Witwicki's verses served as texts for eleven of Chopin's songs for voice and piano, with poems by Bohdan Zaleski and Wincenty

Pol added to the set. Chopin's literary circle was further expanded by many writers he met at Parisian salons, where he was often asked to play and improvise. One of such gatherings was presided over by a celebrated hostess, Juliette Récamier and her lover, François-René Chateaubriand. Madame Récamier's salon guests included Honoré de Balzac, Alphonse de Lamartine, and Charles-Augustin Sainte-Beuve, among others. Chopin also crossed paths with Victor Hugo (1802-1885), whose close friends, Liszt and Berlioz, were also Chopin's companions.

Although many of Chopin's letters were lost in a number of historical misfortunes, those that remain are a fascinating literary expression and provide a tantalizing glimpse of his enigmatic personality. Some of them, especially those addressed to his family and Polish friends, are quite long and have an appearance of the stream-of-consciousness statement. Chopin's language in letters varies from poetic to mundane, and is often very funny and ironic, full of keen observations and insight. On occasion, however, his voice could also be quite sarcastic and mean, particularly when it came to doing business with publishers. Chopin's stratagems of simultaneous negotiating—or delegating Julian Fontana

to deal with the most difficult situations—show his darker, more manipulative side. Towards the end of his life, the tone of Chopin's letters becomes tinged with unspeakable sadness, as in this note to Wojciech Grzymała from London in November 1848:

> [...] I don't need to write you all this, for you know how I think ... [...] Meanwhile, what has become of my art? And my heart, where have I wasted it? I scarcely remember any more how they sing at home. That world slips away from me somehow; I forget, I have no more strength; if I rise a little, I fall again, lower than ever. I am not complaining to you that I am nearer to a coffin than to a marriage bed. My mind is fairly calm.[60]

Chopin was rather reluctant to perform in public and one cannot imagine him giving an impassioned oratory to the crowds. Paderewski on the other hand developed a reputation as an eloquent public speaker whose oratory deeply moved his audiences. Initially, the prospect of addressing the crowd terrified Paderewski almost as much as going on stage to perform in a concert. Public speaking was a skill he did not naturally possess but—as was his habit—he worked on the problem until it was successfully solved. After a series of concerts in Warsaw in 1898, Paderewski delivered an excellent speech that was enthusiastically received by his compatriots but Russian authorities tried to suppress its publication and distribution.[61] In the following years, as he participated in various public functions—especially during the Chopin centennial year in 1910 and when he funded the Battle of Grunwald monument in Kraków—his speaking acquired a vibrant ring of a seasoned orator. In his subsequent political appearances and during a multitude of other civic functions, Paderewski's rhetorical flourishes and cadence became truly heroic. In America, Paderewski made his official debut as a public speaker in 1915 in San Francisco. The war in Europe had devastated Paderewski's homeland since Poland's territory straddled the battlefields of the three neighboring powers, Russia, Germany, and Austria. Paderewski sought to bring humanitarian assistance to Poland and help his country reclaim the long-lost independence. His appeal to the American people opened with a memorable line: "I have to speak about a country which is not yours in a language which is not mine." In 1917 Paderewski addressed Polish-American soldiers preparing to fight for Poland's freedom on the battlefields of Europe:

Go forth to fight the great, the famous battle for Polish soil, for the suffering population, for the whole country under threat! Go forth and prove that courage of old Poland's knights lives in your hearts and that our forefathers' bravery lives on! Go forth and show the world that Polish-Americans are worthy inheritors of Poland's military glory! […] Go forth with faith and courage, proclaiming to all: For Your Freedom and Ours![62]

When Paderewski returned to Poland as Prime Minister of his newly-independent homeland, he spoke to the crowds in Warsaw on 2 January 1919:

I come to you from afar; from across the Ocean I bring you greetings from the four million Poles, whose fate or luck brought them overseas, but who did not forget their homeland. On the contrary, they live and work and think of their beloved Polish soil, where they wholeheartedly want to return. […] I did not return for recognition, fame or awards but to serve. Not to serve a particular party for although I respect them all, I will not join any. There should be only one party—Poland—and I will serve her until the end of my days.[63]

But in private, especially in correspondence to his father and Helena Górska, Paderewski's tone was much lighter, often illuminated with humor and interesting, chatty observations. Most of his other letters tend to be more formal, almost Victorian in its turn of phrase as Paderewski delighted in expressing himself in a very ornate way. Since he was a gifted linguist who spoke several European languages fluently, he wrote equally well in Polish, French and English. Idealistic and noble to the end

Figure 38: The papal nuncio, Paderewski and Herbert Hoover in Warsaw (1919). The Paso Robles Collection, Polish Music Center, USC.

of his days, Paderewski's radio broadcast made shortly after his arrival in New York in 1940 states the guiding principles of his life and charts a course for the world that once again had plunged into the abyss of war:

My dear Friends:
So many of you all over your great and glorious country have whole-heartedly welcomed me during the past fifty years, that I am happy to take this opportunity to offer you my warmest thanks. Since words are inadequate to express my gratitude for your hospitality, your friendship and your affection, I have long ago given you my heart.

The day will come when I will have to part with you; after all it is only natural at my age. Life, the complicated problems it offers, the wisdom of living in order to achieve a full satisfaction in my opinion can be summarized in a few words. Keep on the right path. These words guided me throughout my life and, as I look back, I feel that they represent the only and unfailing principle leading to human perfection. .

In conveying these words to you, I am trying to give you something of lasting value—for everybody is endowed with the more normal moral structure, the demarcation line which means good and evil is firmly established. All one has to do is never to cross that demarcation line in their own direction. Human actions achieved within the right path contribute inevitably to the strengthening and to the development of culture.

The contrary means and will always mean a setback. It certainly is important to individuals as well as to groups of individuals to keep on this path. No considerations, be they social or national, racial or religious, can abolish or even impair this basic fundamental idea even though to some they seem important.

Necessary sufferings could be spared, ruthless wars and endless destruction avoided through the natural striving for perfection. The march of humanity toward general happiness could be assured if everybody would keep on the right path. The problem looks simple, yet it obviously requires a great improvement in human nature before it can be solved. We are still too far from God, and we still, too often, neglect His Commandments. May I be permitted to express my hope and my own ardent conviction, or both, that your great and noble country and my beloved Poland will always, as in their glorious past, remain unshaken champions of truth, of justice, and of good will.[64]

1 See Arthur Rubinstein, *My Young Years,* p. 74-75
2 See Franz Liszt, *Life of Chopin,* p. 59
3 See Helena Modjeska, *Memories and Impressions,* p. 464
4 See Charles Phillips, *Paderewski—The Story of a Modern Immortal,* p. 123
5 See Adam Zamoyski, *Paderewski,* p. 44
6 See James Huneker, *Chopin: The Man and His Music,* p. 51
7 See Jean Jacques Eigeldinger, *Chopin: Pianist and Teacher,* p. 7
8 Ibid., p. 6
9 See Arthur Hedley, *Chopin,* p. 116. Hedley further states that an opera ticket cost twelve francs.
10 Ibid., p. 118
11 See *Chopin's Letters,* p. 195-196
12 See *Paderewski Discovers America* by James H. Phillips, p. 72. The receipts from his second and third American tour reportedly were $160,000 and $248,000, respectively. Also see Rom Landau: *Paderewski,* p. 75
13 See Paderewski and Lawton, *Memoirs,* p. 181-183
14 See *Memoirs* by Paderewski and Lawton, p. 368
15 See *Memoirs* by Paderewski and Lawton, p. 209
16 Ibid., p. 73
17 See Joseph Herter, *Stojowski,* p. 72
18 See *Za kulisami wielkiej kariery* [In the Shadows of a Great Career] by Małgorzata Perkowska-Waszek, pp. 53-54 and 123
19 From an unidentified newspaper clipping in the Zygmunt and Luisa Stojowski Collection Clipping file. Polish Music Center Archives. All rights reserved
20 *Chopin's Letters,* p. 158
21 See Tad Szulc, *Chopin in Paris,* p. 123
22 See *Chopin's Letters,* p. 417
23 Ibid., p. 418
24 From *Memoirs* by Paderewski and Lawton, pp. 56-57
25 Paderewski's son, Alfred, was partially paralyzed and died at the age of twenty-one in 1901
26 See Harold C. Schoenberg, *The Great Pianists,* p. 351
27 See Adam Zamoyski, *Paderewski,* p. 35
28 Ibid., p. 36
29 From *Memoirs* by Paderewski and Lawton, pp. 299-300. Alfred's room was on the ground floor with one of the villa's side entrances, providing quick and easy wheelchair access to the grand marble-paved verandah overlooking the gardens rolling down to Lake Geneva.
30 George Sand (Aurore Dupin-Dudevant) was of noble birth; one of her ancestors was an illegitimate descendant of King Friedrich-August II of Poland and Saxony.
31 See Tad Szulc, *Chopin in Paris,* p. 145
32 Ibid., p. 188
33 Ibid., 189-190
34 *Chopin's Letters,* p. 185
35 Ibid., p. 188-189.

36 Ibid., p. 207

37 See Arthur Hedley, *Chopin*, p. 94-95

38 See Chopin's letter to Grzymała from Nohant dated 29 September 1839

39 *Chopin's Letters*, p. 199

40 See Tad Szulc, *Chopin in Paris*, p. 344

41 See Arthur Hedley, *Chopin*, p. 113

42 See Joseph Herter, *Zygmunt Stojowski—Life and Music*, p. 34

43 Ibid., p. 34

44 See Adam Zamoyski, *Paderewski*, p. 45

45 Ibid., p. 59

46 Ibid., p. 69

47 Ibid., p. 69

48 Helena Paderewska received numerous prizes for her pure-bred chickens and spent enormous sums buying her breeding stock all over the world.

49 From Paderewski's address at the Kosciuszko Foundation Testimonial Dinner at the Hotel Commodore, New York City, May 16, 1928. Zygmunt and Luisa Stojowski Collection, Polish Music Center, USC.

50 From *Memoirs* by Paderewski and Lawton, pp. 391-392

51 The full text of Wilson's Thirteenth Point reads: "The independent Polish state should be erected which should include the territories inhabited by indisputably Polish populations, which should be assured a free and secure access to the sea, and whose political and economic independence and territorial integrity should be guaranteed by international covenant."

52 See Aniela Strakacz, *Paderewski As I Knew Him*, p. 67-68

53 Paderewski's handwritten inscription on a photo in the Paso Robles Collection, Polish Music Center, USC.

54 See Tad Szulc, *Chopin in Paris*, p. 129

55 See *Chopin's Letters*, p. 165-166

56 See Charles Phillips, *Paderewski, the Story of a Modern Immortal*, p. 223

57 See *Chopin's Letters*, p. 131

58 From the unpublished paper, *Ignacy Jan Paderewski: Letters to his Father and Helena Górska*, edited by Małgorzata Perkowska-Waszek and translated by Cara Thornton. Fragment of Paderewski's letter to Helena Górska, 24 May 1886; no. 21 [195]. Used by permission

59 I am very grateful to Paderewski's goddaughter, Anne Appleton-Strakacz, who augmented the existing photos of Riond-Bosson with her detailed commentary and explanations of the house, its master, and the furnishings inside.

60 Ibid., p. 397

61 Ibid. p. 231

62 See Franciszek Pulit, *Dom w ojczyźnie*, p.100

63 Ibid., p. 100

64 From a typed, undated transcript, "Paderewski Speech; Record Number 1 (The Right Path)" found in the Zygmunt and Luisa Stojowski Collection, Polish Music Center Archives, USC

Chapter Seven

The Polish Piano School

The lives of Chopin and Paderewski were permeated by their strong attachment to the cause of Poland's independence. During the early decades of the nineteenth century the memories of Poland's glorious past and of the democratic fervor that brought Poland's 1791 Constitution were still alive. The tragic ending of the Kościuszko Uprising in 1794 and the final round of partitioning Poland's territory among her neighbors at the end of the eighteenth century continued to weigh heavily on the minds of the generation of Chopin's parents. Poles who came of age during the first two decades of the nineteenth century were the first to be raised in a partitioned country, where the three occupying regimes—Prussia, Russia, and Austria—set strict limits on personal, political and cultural freedoms. Given harsh repressions that followed any public expression of national identity, the hopes for Poland's survival depended on the individual preservation of Polish language, customs, and culture. This mission was paramount across all levels of society and parents of each succeeding generation felt obligated to inculcate the young with their own concept of Polish nationality and history.

For over a century to all of her subjects, Poland was only an abstract, ephemeral entity maintained in the collective consciousness often under extremely adverse conditions. Censorship—be it Russian, Prussian or Austrian—within carefully controlled schools, newspapers, and literary efforts forced Poles to use the language of the occupying force in all official communications. Freedom of movement was strongly restricted, with passports and various permits required for travel across what was once a sovereign territory. In the areas of Poland administered by the Russian authorities the repressions were especially severe. Warsaw—once the open and cosmopolitan capital of Poland—became a provincial Russian town, where cultural and political dissent was methodically annihilated by the tsarist police apparatus. In addition to imprisonment, dissidents risked banishment for many years to remote regions of Siberia as well as confiscation of property. Many universities were either closed or placed under the supervision of secret police and, as a result, a number of leading intellectual and political activists were forced into exile.

Chopin's strong sense of national pride surfaced already in his childhood and his lively interest in the Polish countryside and its music had inspired his earliest compositions. Visiting Vienna in 1828, the eighteen-year old Chopin reported with great indignation to his friend Jan Matuszyński the negative opinion of Poland expressed by the Austrian public:

Today, at dinner in the Italian restaurant I heard: *Der liebe Gott hat einen Fehler gemacht, dass er die Polen geschaffen hat*; so don't wonder if I can't express what I feel. Don't expect to hear any news from a Pole, after hearing another man answer: *In Polen ist Nichts zu holen.* The curs![1]

The young Polish intelligentsia was just as resentful of the political situation in Russian-administered Warsaw and many of Chopin's closest friends actively participated in the November Uprising of 1830 in the capital. When the insurrection was brutally suppressed by the Russians, the news of the fall of Warsaw provoked an angry outburst from Chopin; the entry in his diary written in Stuttgart in September of 1831 betrays an extraordinary agitation, despair, despondency, wrath, and resignation:

The clocks in the towers of Stuttgart strike the hours of the night. How many new corpses is this minute making in the world? Mothers losing children, children losing mothers—So much grief over the dead, and so much delight! […] I am right to be angry that I came into the world—What use is my existence to anyone? […] Father! Mother! Where are you? Corpses? Perhaps some Russian has played tricks—[…] For a moment I died in my heart; no, my heart died in me for a moment. Ah, why not for ever!—Perhaps it would be more endurable then—Alone! Alone!—There are no words for my misery; how can I bear this feeling—[2]

For the rest of his life, Chopin's intense feelings regarding his homeland were passionately echoed in several of his compositions. One can argue that his Mazurkas, Polonaises, and Ballades—compositions permeated with a strongly Polish subtext—represent Chopin's patriotic response to the historical tragedy that befell his beloved country. The noble pride of his Polonaises, the touching verity of the folk idiom in the Mazurkas, and the palpable sense of the poetic narrative in the Ballades all manifest Chopin's profound kinship with the history and traditions of Poland.

As soon as Chopin settled in Paris, he quickly befriended a number of Poles residing there. For most of the Polish nobility and intelligentsia who were raised speaking Polish and French and deeply enamored of the French culture, Paris was the only conceivable destination for an exile. But Polish émigrés in Paris were a large and diverse group, consisting of not only of the aristocratic elite and artists of all kinds, but also of professionals, tradesmen, former soldiers and revolutionaries, and some of the working class. The Czartoryskis with their opulent Hôtel Lambert on Île Saint-Louis were at the summit of Polish society in Paris, but many of their compatriots lived in great poverty in the so-called "little Poland" section of Paris near Gare Saint-Lazare. In his September 1831 letter, Chopin remarked that the "number of Poles here is inconceivable."[3] The rapid increase of Polish immigrants notwithstanding, most Parisians were generally sympathetic to the Polish cause. Poet Victor Hugo, General Lafayette (Commander of the French National Guard), and several members of the French parliament condemned the brutality of Russian intervention in Warsaw. But the political status quo of the partitions remained and Poles of all kinds continued to stream to Paris. The more fortunate émigrés tried to help the new, often destitute arrivals, and Chopin frequently participated in various relief actions for the Polish cause. Nonetheless, unlike his friend Adam Mickiewicz and other prominent exile figures, Chopin usually refrained from making public political statements. Liszt—whose recollections of Chopin are not always balanced or reliable—recalled that in matters political Chopin kept his own counsel:

His patriotism was revealed in the course taken by his genius, in the choice of his friends, in the preferences given to pupils, and in the frequent and great services which he rendered to his compatriots; but we cannot remember that he took any pleasure in the expression of this feeling. If he sometimes entered upon the topic of politics, so vividly attacked, so warmly defended, so frequently discussed in France, it was rather to point out what he deemed dangerous or erroneous in the opinions advanced by others than to win attention for his own. In constant connection with some of the most brilliant politicians of the day, he knew how to limit the relations between them to a personal attachment entirely independent of political interests. [...] He followed at a distance the progress of events, and an acuteness of perception, which he would scarcely have been supposed to possess, often enabled him to predict occurrences which were not anticipated even by the best informed. [...] His concise remarks attracted no attention until time proved their truth.[4]

Unlike Chopin, a good part of Paderewski's life was spent in politics, and his achievements in this area were on a historical scale. The turning point came during 1910, a year devoted to the celebrations of Chopin's centennial and the five hundredth anniversary of the Battle of Grunwald, where Polish and Lithuanian troops defeated the Knights of the Teutonic Order. Paderewski prominently participated in a number of commemorative events in Poland connected to both occasions. In addition he funded—entirely from his own pocket—and supervised the design of the majestic Battle of Grunwald monument in Kraków. Travelling largely through the Austrian part of Poland, where political restrictions were the mildest, Paderewski delivered many patriotic speeches and was enthusiastically received by his fellow Poles. Always well informed about current affairs and close to the ruling elites of Europe and America, Paderewski sensed that he was finally able to advocate the cause of Poland's independence, a goal that preoccupied him from his early childhood onwards. Like no other politician in the history of his country, Paderewski actually succeeded in full when after World War I Poland became a free and democratic state for twenty years. When Hitler and Stalin invaded Poland in September 1939, Paderewski's life's work was in ruins and once more he had to help his beloved land. In spite of frail health, he sprang to battle, making radio broadcasts and renewing his worldwide appeals to help Poland. He traveled to Geneva to represent Polish interests at the League of Nations. In January 1940 he became President of the National Council in exile. Unfortunately, Paderewski's valiant efforts had little success this time around: Poland was a defeated country, suffering terrible hardships under a Nazi and Soviet occupation, and the political and military situation in Europe continued to worsen from month to month. The last year of Paderewski's life, when once again he was in the United States, was once more devoted to a tireless campaign of rallying support of the Allies to the Polish cause.

Prominent historical factors present in the lives of Chopin and Paderewski both influenced and, in large measure, defined their musical legacy. The opening line of the national anthem, *Jeszcze Polska nie zginęła* [Poland has not perished yet], forged in the early campaigns for Poland's independence at the beginning of the nineteenth century, became for Chopin and Paderewski an artistic motto and personal *cri de coeur*. To the casual European observer, Chopin's and Paderewski's homeland, absorbed into Prussia, Russia, and Austria, seemed doomed and lost. The Polish spirit and culture—so the partitioning powers had hoped—would eventually be subjugated and subsumed into the prevailing customs of the administrators of this once proud and prosperous republic. Against such background, Chopin's strongly patriotic compositions, public and private concerts, participation in various émigré activities, as well as his great prominence in exile, delivered strong proof to the world and to the inhabitants of the ccupied homeland that indeed Poland "has not perished yet."

Paderewski's skyrocketing fame and worldwide celebrity after his Paris debut, the enormous amount of public concerts he gave before World War I, his public speaking in Poland during important anniversary celebrations, and his outstanding public advocacy in America for Poland's independence, were just as strong an indication that Poland and Polish culture continue to exist and thrive, in spite of limits placed on expressions of national heritage.

Chopin's recitals as well as those of Paderewski and other well-known pianists who dedicated their programs to Chopin's compositions, not only fortified the message that Poland "has not perished yet" but also contributed to the establishment of the foundations for the so-called "Polish School" of piano playing. It includes such performance characteristics as a strongly-felt rhythmic temperament taken partially from Polish folk music traditions and the poetic application of a flexible musical flow, the so-called *tempo rubato*. It also suggests a degree of identification and sympathy with Poland's history, heritage and literature. These attributes were and continue to be among the *sine qua non* requirements for interpreting Chopin's music. Besides innovations in applying fingering and modernizing of practice methods, the technical side of piano performance bequeathed by Chopin to his disciples and their students included a rounded and singing tone, transparence and clarity of execution, effortless and natural delivery, depth of musical feeling without the sense of exaggeration, elegant differentiation between the melodic lines and the accompaniment, truly original use of pedal, secure sense of formal design, and strong grasp of the musical purpose in the works performed. By extension, these characteristics became associated with the Polish Piano School as well.

This tradition was passed to succeeding generations of pianists by some of Chopin's long-time students, including Karol Mikuli, Georges-Amédée-Saint-Clair Mathias, and Camille O'Meara-Dubois. Of Polish-Armenian ancestry, Mikuli was born in Czerniowce and came to Paris to study with Chopin during the years 1844-1848. His piano apprenticeship with Chopin was highly significant since Mikuli became Chopin's assistant, observing other pupils' lessons and filling in at times as Chopin's official copyist. After concertizing throughout Europe, Mikuli became a professor of piano, harmony and counterpoint at the Music Conservatory in Lwów in 1858. His most enduring accomplishment in preserving Chopin's legacy was to publish a seventeen-volume collection of Chopin's music in 1880, based on the original French editions published during Chopin's lifetime. These he annotated not only with marks entered during his own lessons but also with comments, fingering, and other interpretative guidelines given by Chopin to his other students, including Princess

Figure 39: Unknown artist: Karol Mikuli, oil on board, 19th century. Collection of the Frederic Chopin Museum at the Frederic Chopin National Institute. Owned by the Frederic Chopin Society, M/2619. Used by permission

Czartoryska, Madame Dubois, Madame Rubio, and Madame Streicher-Müller. Additional observations by Chopin's friends and musical collaborators, such as Ferdinand Hiller and Auguste Franchomme, also found their way into Mikuli's authoritative and monumental work. Several of Mikuli's students from Lwów went on to significant concert and teaching careers, including Aleksander Michałowski (1851-1938), Maurycy Rosenthal (1862-1946), and Raoul Koczalski (1884-1948). A few recordings by Michałowski and many more by Rosenthal and Koczalski contain some fascinating interpretations and give tantalizing clues to Chopin's style of playing.

Georges Mathias was Chopin's student for at least six years and was universally recognized as a child prodigy. After visiting with the thirteen-year old Mathias in Paris, German virtuoso Clara Wieck (who later became Schumann's wife) reported to her father in March of 1839:

You should hear this child, an immense talent, a pupil of Chopin. How can I describe his gifts? You know about child prodigies; I should only add that this one has received an excellent education, has wonderfully flexible fingers, plays all of Chopin, and there is nothing he cannot do. In fact he outshines all the keyboard strummers around here. [...] I was to give him lessons, but I told him he had no need of a teacher. (You know, I would be too afraid to teach him, since his mental abilities exceed his physical abilities.) I played duets with him and I plan to visit this family often, especially as I shall be living quite near them.[5]

Beginning in 1862 Mathias became a professor of piano at the Paris Conservatoire and during his tenure of thirty years trained a great number of French pianists in the Chopin tradition. Among Mathias' students were such notable virtuosos as Raoul Pugno (1852-1914), Teresa Carreño (1853-1917), Isidor Phillip (1863-1958), and Ernest Schelling (1876-1939), the latter a close friend of Paderewski who often visited him in Switzerland.

Along with Mathias, Camille O'Meara-Dubois was one of Chopin's best and most talented students. She commenced working with Chopin in 1843 when she was thirteen and studied with him for five years. Many of Chopin's closest friends and long-time students agreed that she was his favorite pupil. In the last year of studying with Chopin, she also became his assistant and later performed in concert with Chopin's chamber music partners, the violinist Alard and cellist Franchomme. Her playing was described as "fine, delicate, and distinguished, like that of her illustrious teacher," and Chopin's student, Jane Stirling, remarked in the 1851 letter to Chopin's sister: "I've heard Mlle Meara, whose playing is a good as ever. I ardently wish her to preserve the tradition."[6] Liszt referred to Madame O'Meara-Dubois as the authority on Chopin; Paderewski, whose Parisian debut she witnessed in 1888, wrote that:

She must have been in her youth extremely beautiful, because when I introduced to her for the first time, she was already a very old lady but of exceptionally attractive features and beautiful expression. […] Madame Dubois was the mother of all the pianists in the best Parisian society![7]

Madame Dubois' other important contribution to preserving Chopin's musical legacy was the donation of scores used for her lessons to the Bibliothèque Nationale in Paris. She first gave them to the French pianist, Louis Diémer, and stipulated that they be later deposited at the Bibliothèque Nationale.[8] The four volumes of Chopin's music from Madame Dubois contain numerous pencil annotations by Chopin, fingerings, dynamic markings, textual corrections and occasional additions of musical material, interpretative remarks and many other priceless indications of Chopin's wishes regarding the performance of his music.

There were also many of Chopin's friends, associates, acquaintances and contemporaries who performed and popularized Chopin's opus in concerts. Julian Fontana, Ferdinand Hiller, Franz Liszt, Anton Rubinstein, and Louis Moreau Gottschalk were just a few of the most prominent pianists who were at the core of the rapidly-expanding group of "Chopinists" as Chopin's music continued to find appreciative audiences and dedicated performers.

Unlike Chopin, Paderewski was a rather reluctant teacher with only a few outstanding disciples. Zygmunt Stojowski was the most prominent among them, as he went on to a very respectable career as a touring pianist and a noted composer. The two had met in Kraków well before Paderewski's Parisian debut. Shortly thereafter Stojowski continued

Figure 40: Zygmunt Stojowski in 1910. Zygmunt and Luisa Stojowski Collection, Polish Music Center, USC.

on to Paris, where studied piano with Louis Diémer (a Dubois-Chopin connection!) and composition with Léo Delibes. Stojowski and Paderewski remained lifelong friends and Paderewski invariably recommended Stojowski as an excellent piano teacher after his younger colleague settled in New York City in 1905. Among Paderewski's occasional students in the early days of his career were Antonina Szumowska (1868-1938), Harold Bauer (1873-1951) and Ernest Schelling. Towards the end of his life Paderewski agreed to mentor the most promising young Polish pianists and in 1928 agreed to invite them for a summer session of master classes at his Swiss residence. These informal workshops continued annually until 1932 and included Aleksander Brachocki (1897-1948), Zygmunt Dygat (1894-1977), Stanisław Szpinalski (1901-1957), Henryk Sztompka (1901-1964), and Albert Tadlewski (1892-1945). Witold Małcużyński (1914-1977) and Józef Turczyński (1884-1953) also benefited from a few lessons with Paderewski in the late 1930s and were his last piano students.

According to Zygmunt Dygat, Paderewski's students arrived in Switzerland at the beginning of the summer and had their lessons on Saturday afternoons. Paderewski was very through in his teaching and devoted long hours to the task. At the end of the day all students were invited to an excellent meal and vintage wine at Paderewski's residence and treated to an unforgettable evening of storytelling by the Master.[9]

From among this small group only Stanisław Szpinalski and Witold Małcużyński became internationally recognized pianists. Szpinalski received the Second Prize at the 1932 Chopin Competition in Warsaw and performed extensively in Europe and the United States before and after World War II, specializing in traditional as well as contemporary music repertoire. During the war years, Szpinalski taught at the Music Conservatory in Wilno. Although his postwar career was cut short by pancreatic cancer, Szpinalski nonetheless edited a number of piano works by Paderewski and modern Polish composers and left a small catalogue of excellent recordings.

Witold Małcużyński was the Third Prize winner at the 1937 Chopin Competition and thereafter lived in France and the United States. Respected as an insightful interpreter of Chopin, Małcużyński concertized extensively around the world and made a number of recordings for the Columbia label in England. In 1946

Figure 41: Paderewski's students in Switzerland (left to right), Zygmunt Dygat, Albert Tadlewski, Henryk Sztompka, and Stanisław Leopold Szpinalski. Silvio, Paderewski's chauffeur, stands next to the Cadillac limousine. Private Collection. Used by permission. All rights reserved

Małcużyński recorded a recital for the BBC on the piano used by Chopin during his last visit to London in 1848.

Chopin and Paderewski defined the Romantic style of piano playing by cultivating an approach that strove to produce a singing, penetrating and beautiful tone that was also supported by their pioneering use of pedal effects. This in turn helped uncover properties that made the piano capable of charming the audience with sounds and colors that ranged from intimate whispers to full orchestral thunder. In their performances Chopin and Paderewski always relied on elegant touch and an interpretation unencumbered by theatrical displays of any kind. Considering the well-known stage antics of Liszt, Paganini, and de Pachmann to name but a few, the calm musical delivery given first by Chopin and Paderewski represented a revolutionary concept at the time.

Whilst the effect of Chopin's performances could only be described in various testimonials by his friends and students, Paderewski's magisterial virtuosity, penetrating tone and magnificently structured interpretations can be found not only in some of his early sound recordings but also on film. It is indeed remarkable to watch Paderewski—then in his late seventies—deliver with majestic nobility and admirable bravura a truly breathtaking performance of works by Beethoven, Chopin, and Liszt in the film *Moonlight Sonata*.

With their rich legacy of deeply inspired pianism that opened new expressive horizons, Chopin and Paderewski influenced generations of artists worldwide and the list of pianists who are associated with continuing their legacy is very long indeed. Although Liszt is credited with inventing the solo piano recital, in the course of their careers Chopin and Paderewski succeeded in defining the piano recital as an intimate, poetic, and life-changing experience for their audiences. Their spellbinding ways of communicating with the public through music still serve as an inspiration to every performing artist. To this day, almost the entire repertoire of Chopin music regularly appears on concert stages and shows no signs of fading with age. For many, Chopin's music is a benchmark for judging each pianist's musicianship, interpretative skills, and technical accomplishment.

Recognizing Chopin's contributions to the history of Polish music began in earnest at the time of the centennial celebrations of his birth in 1910. Paderewski was at the forefront of a number of important events, especially in Lwów, where he delivered a widely-publicised speech on Chopin and the meaning of his music in Poland's history:

Shortly after Chopin's departure, his homeland—especially the farthest of provinces—came under terrible and widely known repressions; such repressions whose exemplary brutality can be explained only by some thoughtless, wild revenge exacted upon the innocent for their long servitude under the Tatars. Everything was forbidden to us! – the language of our fathers, the faith of our forefathers, the worship of holy events from our past, our costumes, customs, and our nation's songs… They forbade us Słowacki, Krasiński, Mickiewicz. But they did not forbid us Chopin. And in Chopin we have everything that was forbidden: colorful robes, gold-studded belt buckles, sober grey long-coats, festive Cracovian hats, the din of nobles' swords, the gleam of peasants' scythes, the groans of the wounded hearts, the revolts of caged spirits, cemetery crosses, wayside chapels, prayers of worried hearts, pains of imprisonment, longing for freedom, cursing of tyrants, and joyous songs of liberty. For many years of suffering, torture and discrimination, for many years the threads of our forbidden and most secret thoughts reached out to him, and our pain-filled hearts sought his comfort. And lo, how many he had comforted and fortified… and maybe even converted. For it was he, the smuggler who in the rolled up scores of innocent notes delivered this forbidden Poland to his compatriots scattered in the far provinces; for it again was he, the chaplain who supplied us the holy sacraments of our Homeland.

He now stands up in glamour of his earthly glory, in the immortal rays of the whole nation's gratitude, covered in wreaths of freshest laurel, braided with love and adulation. But he stands not alone… "Genius Patrie," the spirit of the native land does not abandon him, not even in his death…

A great man, even the greatest, cannot stand above or away from the nation. He is the seed, its particle, its flower, and its fruition—and the bigger or finer, the closer is he to the heart of the nation… Chopin may not have known his greatness. But this we know, as his greatness is ours, his strength—our power, his beauty—our reflection. He is ours and we are his, as our collective soul remains within his being.

Let us strengthen our hearts to continue and overcome; let us tailor our thoughts to our brave and just goals, and let our feelings lift our strong faith, because a nation that has such great and immortal soul will never perish.[10]

Continuing on this path of commemorating Poland's greatest composer, in 1937 Paderewski together with Ludwik Bronarski (1890-1975) and Józef Turczyński began the monumental task of publishing a critical edition of Chopin's compositions that was intended to commemorate the centennial of Chopin's death in 1949. The outbreak of World War II in 1939 and Paderewski's death in 1941 caused the project to be delayed. It was finally published in twenty-one volumes during the years 1949-1961 and this set of scores—bearing Paderewski's name as chief editor and henceforth known as the "Paderewski Edition"—still represents the most authoritative source on Chopin's music.

In the meantime Jerzy Żurawlew (1887-1980), a favourite student of Aleksander Michałowski, organized the first international Chopin Piano Competition in Warsaw in 1927. Held every five years in the Polish capital (with a break during World War II), the Competition launched the careers of many distinguished pianists, including Lev Oborin, Stanisław Szpinalski, Witold Małcużyński, Bella Davidovitch, Halina Czerny-Stefańska, Barbara Hesse-Bukowska, Adam Harasiewicz, Vladimir Ashkenazy, Bernard Ringeissen, Maurizio Pollini, Martha Argerich, Arturo Moreira-Lima, Garrick Ohlsson, Piotr Paleczny, Krystian Zimerman, Kevin Kenner, and Rafał Blechacz, among many others.

One of many tributes to the Polish Piano School was provided by the Steinway & Sons piano company in their 1930s campaign, "The Instrument of the Immortals." The advertisement represents the greatest pianists of the era, with Paderewski reigning supreme at the top of the list. Besides him there are several other great Polish pianists and Paderewski's close friends, including Józef Hofmann (1876-1957), Zygmunt Stojowski, and Ernest Schelling.

In addition to those listed above, a number of other Polish-born pianists with strong connections to Chopin's school are also listed in this Steinway brochure. Ignacy Friedman (1882-1948), born in Kraków, was a brilliant virtuoso and a gifted composer. His 1904 debut in Vienna included three piano concertos and dozens of encores. Like Paderewski, Friedman studied with Leschetizky. Friedman's concert repertoire was vast and he gave numerous concerts all over the world. At the outset of World War II he fled to Australia, where he spent his last years.

Wanda Landowska (1879-1959) was born in Warsaw, where she studied piano with Aleksander Michałowski. She eventually became a famous harpsichordist, whose pioneering research into Baroque-era music and old instruments led to the present day interest in period-style performance practice.

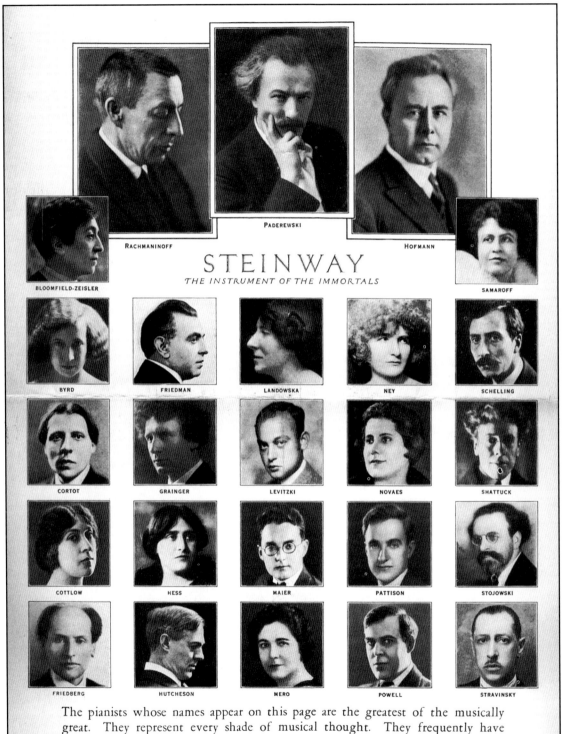

RACHMANINOFF

PADEREWSKI

HOFMANN

BLOOMFIELD-ZEISLER

SAMAROFF

STEINWAY
THE INSTRUMENT OF THE IMMORTALS

BYRD   FRIEDMAN   LANDOWSKA   NEY   SCHELLING

CORTOT   GRAINGER   LEVITZKI   NOVAES   SHATTUCK

COTTLOW   HESS   MAIER   PATTISON   STOJOWSKI

FRIEDBERG   HUTCHESON   MERO   POWELL   STRAVINSKY

The pianists whose names appear on this page are the greatest of the musically great. They represent every shade of musical thought. They frequently have sharply contrasted ideas. They unite, however, in one common conviction — their belief in the unquestioned superiority of the Steinway piano.

Figure 42: Archives of the Polish Music Center, USC.

Like Paderewski, she studied with Heinrich Urban in Berlin, and later taught harpsichord at the Berlin Musik Hochschule. Landowska then moved to Paris, where her influence on the musical life was a considerable: Manuel de Falla and Francis Poulenc wrote harpsichord concertos for her. She fled from France in 1940, reaching New York on December 7, 1941, the day of Pearl Harbor attack. Afterwards she settled in Connecticut, teaching, recording and writing about music until the end of her life.

Mischa Lewitzki (1898-1941), born in the Ukraine, also studied with Michałowski in Warsaw and from 1906-1911 was a pupil of Stojowski at the Institute of Musical Arts in New York City. Known for his sparkling technique, he toured extensively around the world, but settled and died in the United States.

Other important pianists listed in the Steinway advertisement include Alfred Cortot (1877-1962), and Guiomar Novaes (1895-1979). Although not Polish by heritage, these torch-bearers of the Chopin tradition carried on the legacy of the Polish Piano School. Cortot was a pupil of Diémer in Paris, and is mainly remembered for his inspired interpretations and recordings of Chopin's music. Cortot also extensively annotated many of Chopin's works with performance guidance, fingering and exercises designed to overcome technical difficulties. Cortot's editions of Chopin are still quite popular among many aspiring piano students. Novaes began studying piano in her native Brazil but travelled to Paris to study with Isidor Phillip at the Conservatoire. Through Phillip and his teacher, Mathias, Novaes represented the third generation of pianists directly linked to the Chopin tradition. During her long career Novaes also studied with Stojowski and recorded a large Chopin repertoire on the VOX label in the United States in the 1950s.

It was indeed quite fitting for Steinway & Sons to place Paderewski on top of the list of "Steinway Immortals," right next to two other keyboard giants, Sergei Rachmaninov and Józef Hofmann. At the summit of his long and distinguished career, Paderewski's exalted position in the pantheon of pianists has been secured not only by his musical genius, sterling character, and the unprecedented generosity towards mankind, but mainly because of his profound connection to the music of Frederic Chopin.

1 See *Chopin's Letters*, p. 133. These two German sayings can be translated as, "A mistake was made by good God, when he hath Poles begat" and "Poland is nothing, a no-land." [MZ]
2 See *Chopin's Letters*, p. 149-150
3 Ibid., p. 151.
4 See Franz Liszt, *Life of Chopin*, p. 81-82
5 See Jean-Jacques Eigeldinger, Chopin: *Pianist and Teacher*, p. 170.
6 Ibid., p. 164.
7 See Paderewski and Lawton, *Memoirs*, p. 142
8 Louis-Joseph Diémer (1843-1919) studied piano at the Paris Conservatoire with Antoine Marmontel (1816-1898), who was one of Chopin's good friends in Paris and owned Chopin's portrait made by Delacroix.
9 See Zygmunt Dygat's reminiscences of studying with Paderewski in his article for the May-June 1935 issue of *Echo Muzyczne i Teatralne*.
10 From Paderewski's speech, *O Szopenie* [About Chopin] delivered at the centennial celebrations of Chopin in Lwów, 23 October 1910. Published in Lwów, 1911. Collection of the Polish Music Center. All rights reserved. Translation by the author.

~ ACKNOWLEDGMENTS ~

As this book was gradually taking shape over the past few months, its author had the distinct pleasure of being on the receiving end of much-needed assistance from a variety of sources all over the world. The biggest share of thanks goes to Krysta Close and Daniel Kamiński, two of my associates (and dear friends) at the Polish Music Center, University of Southern California. Krysta very kindly surveyed the entire manuscript and provided many useful editorial and content suggestions, whilst Daniel carefully scanned a number of documents held in the Polish Music Center's archives that are reproduced in this book.

Heartfelt hospitality graciously extended over the past few months by various friends of mine was another important factor that enabled me to complete my intellectual task. In the early weeks of the writing process I was a guest of my long-time London friends, Dr. Zbigniew Szydło, his wife, Dr. Lidia Tyszczuk, and their delightful family. Ensconced in a quiet room in their spacious north London house I could enjoy much peace and some inspiration, as I looked out over the majestic treetops of Highgate's Queen's Wood and distant silhouettes of London's landmarks set against pale, wintry light. My other dear London friends, Dr. Charles Jonscher, his wife Renata, and their children, hosted me for several excellent meals in their palatial surroundings, nurturing and nourishing me with the greatest and kindest care only they know how to dispense; their hospitality was truly regal and so is my gratitude.

Afterwards, among the sun-splashed hillsides of California's Central Coast, I was a guest of Steve and Alice Cass—great friends and even greater fans of Ignacy Jan Paderewski, who live among picturesque vineyards on the east side of the charming town of Paso Robles. Their spacious house and a fine Steinway piano—plus a quiet guestroom overlooking the stunning landscape that turned verdant green with spring rains—provided another perfect place where I could continue with my task. Excellent meals that Alice prepared and superb wines from

Steve's vineyard provided much of the urgently needed sustenance for this project. Visiting Paso Robles, where Paderewski's footsteps still resonate in the community's collective memory and his spirit is kept alive by an excellent annual music festival, made me experience first hand that part of Paderewski's own story that I later tried to convey on these pages.

My grateful acknowledgment also extends to the entire staff of the Department of Cultural and Public Diplomacy in the Ministry of Foreign Affairs in Warsaw. Their enthusiasm and material support for *Celebrating Chopin and Paderewski* was just as important as their initial suggestion that this book be written in commemoration of two momentous anniversaries in the history of Polish music. The Ministry's representatives in California—the Consulate General of the Republic of Poland in Los Angeles—were also partners in this enterprise and I appreciate the assistance they had so kindly provided.

Among my West Coast friends, I would also like to thank Anne Appleton-Strakacz, Antoinette Bower, Charles and Alice Bragg, Jann Castor, Bartosz Chmielowski, Patryk Dawid Chlastawa, Wallace Cunningham, Yola Czaderska-Hayek, Betty Harford, Thomas Hien, Amanda Horton, Jack Larson, David Lynch, Danuta Rothschild, Stefan Wenta, and Bart Ziegler for their understanding; all too often they had to endure my constant refrain, "Please let me finish my book first!" whenever they inquired about my well-being. I hope their patience will be at least partially rewarded by what they find between the covers of this little volume.

From among my friends in Poland, most importantly Marek Żydowicz and the staff of the Tumult Foundation, the organizers of the Plus Camerimage Film Festival, deserve to be recognized for their unwavering support of all of my creative enterprises over the past several years. Dr. Małgorzata Perkowska, the greatest expert in the world on Paderewski and a valued friend, contributed much of her encyclopedic knowledge, materials and expertise to this book. Her generous assistance radiates from every page devoted to Paderewski in this essay. My brother Piotr-Tomasz, now living in Poland, often served as my ad-hoc consultant, host, and research assistant. Helping out a brother in need is often one of those thankless family tasks, but he fulfilled it with much grace and goodwill. In addition, during the past two years, I was able to make new and enduring friends in the province of Tarnów, where Paderewski himself resided at the very end of the nineteenth century. Mieczysław Kras, Supervisor of the Tarnów District, Ryszard Żądło, President of Tarnów City Council, and Madame Krystyna Szymańska, Director of the Paderewski Center Tarnów-Kąśna Dolna extended exemplary Polish hospitality and cordial friendship without which this book could not come to be.

Finally, as I contemplated the art of piano playing whilst writing these pages, I also thought quite often of my mother, Kamilla. Although she made her career in law, she first studied voice and piano at the Wilno Conservatory in Poland. She was the first to encourage me to take piano lessons when I was five and in her resolve she was supported by a close family friend, Stanisław Leopold Szpinalski—a brilliant pianist and one of the very few prominent students of Paderewski. Over several decades, my other teachers and mentors—Irena Marczykowska, Zbigniew Świeżyński, Olga Iliwicka-Dąbrowska, Robert Casadesus, Nadia Boulanger, and Russell Sherman—had contributed to my understanding of the great and noble pianistic tradition. Each piece of music that I have studied under their guidance has opened new interpretative horizons, and their precious insights regarding especially the piano music of Chopin and Paderewski are hereby gratefully acknowledged.

M.Ż.

Selected Bibliography

Atwood, William, G. *The Parisian Worlds of Frederic Chopin*. Yale University Press, New Haven and London, 1999

Bauer, Harold. *His Book*. W.W. Norton & Company, Inc. New York 1948

Bonsal, Stephen. *Suitors and Supplicants—The Little Nations at Versailles*. Prentice-Hall, Inc., New York, 1946

Chopin, Frederic. *Chopin's Letters*. Collected by Henryk Opieński. Vienna House, New York, 1973

Davies, Norman. *God's Playground, a History of Poland in Two Volumes*. Columbia University Press, New York, 1982

Dobrzański, Sławomir. *Maria Szymanowska—Pianist and Composer*. Figueroa Press, 2006

Drozdowski, Marian Marek. *Ignacy Jan Paderewski—A Political Biography in Outline*. Interpress, 1981

Dulęba, Władysław & Sokołowska, Zofia. *Paderewski*. The Kosciuszko Foundation, New York, and PWM Edition, Kraków, 1979

Eigeldinger, Jean-Jacques. *Chopin: Pianist and Teacher As Seen by His Pupils*. Cambridge University Press, 2008

Einstein, Alfred. *Music in the Romantic Era*. W. W. Norton & Company, Inc. New York, 1947

Eisler, Benita. *Chopin's Funeral*. Vintage Books—Random House, Inc. New York, 2003

Finck, Henry T. *Paderewski and His Art*. Whittingham & Atherton, New York 1895

Gavoty, Bernard. *Frederic Chopin*. Translated from the French by Martin Sokolinsky. Charles Scribner's Sons, New York, 1977

Gottschalk, Louis Moreau. *Notes of a Pianist*. Princeton University Press. Princeton and Oxford, 2006

Gronowicz, Antoni. *Paderewski, Pianist and Patriot*. Thomas Nelson & Sons, Edinburgh, New York, Toronto, 1943

Hedley, Arthur. *Chopin*. Collier Books, New York, N.Y., 1962

Herter, Joseph A. *Zygmunt Stojowski—Life and Music*. Figueroa Press, Los Angeles, 2007

Huneker, James. *Chopin: The Man and His Music*. Dover Publications, New York, 1966

Huneker, James. *Franz Liszt*. Scribner's Sons, New York, 1911

Iwaszkiewicz, Jarosław. *Chopin*. Polskie Wydawnictwo Muzyczne, 1966

Iwaszkiewicz, Jarosław. *Żelazowa Wola*. Wydawnictwo Sport i Turystyka, Warszawa, 1965

Jeżewska, Zofia. *Fryderyk Chopin*. Wydawnictwo Interpress. Warszawa, 1969

Kellogg, Charlotte. *Paderewski*. The Viking Press, New York, 1956

Landau, Rom. *Paderewski*. Ivor Nicholson & Watson, Ltd. London, 1934

Lengyel, Emil. *Ignace Paderewski, Musician and Statesman*. Franklin Watts, Inc., New York, 1970

Liszt, Franz. *Life of Chopin*. Forgotten Books, Lexington KY 2010

March, Francis A. *History of the World War*. The United Publishers of the United States and Canada. Philadelphia, Chicago, Toronto, 1919.

Marchwica, Wojciech Maria, and Sitarz, Andrzej, Editors. *Warsztat kompozytorski, wykonawstwo, koncepcje polityczne Ignacego Jana Paderewskiego* [The Compositional Skill, Performances, and Political Ideas of Ignacy Jan Paderewski]. Musica Jagiellonica, Kraków 1991

Marek, George R. and Gordon-Smith, Maria. *Chopin*. Harper & Row, Publishers, New York, Hagerstown, San Francisco, London, 1978

Mayzner, Tadeusz. *Chopin*. Polskie Wydawnictwo Muzyczne, 1968

McGinty, Brian. *Paderewski at Paso Robles*. Overland Books, 2004

McMillan, Mary Lee & Jones, Ruth Dorval. *My Helenka*. Moore Publishing Company, Durham, NC, 1972

Modjeska, Helena. *Memories and Impressions of Helena Modjeska, An Autobiography*. The MacMillan Company, New York, 1910

Morawińska, Agnieszka. *Chopin and the Art of His Time*. Published in the Composers and the Art of Their Time. Adam Mickiewicz Institute, Warsaw, 2005

Niecks, Frederick. *Frederick Chopin As a Man and Musician*. Novello and Company, London, Third Edition, 1902

Ochlewski, Tadeusz, Ed. *Dzieje muzyki polskiej* [The History of Polish Music]. Wydawnictwo Interpress, Warszawa, 1977

Opieński, Henryk. *Chopin*. Altenberg Publishing, Lwów, & Wende i Spółka Publishing, Warsaw, 1909

Opieński, Henryk. *Ignacy Jan Paderewski*. Gebethner & Wolff, Warszawa, 1928

Orłowski, Józef, Dr. *Helena Paderewska—Na piętnastolecie Jej pracy narodowej i społecznej*, 1914-1929 [Helena Paderewska—On the Fifteenth Anniversary of Her National and Civic Service], Chicago Illinois, 1929

Orłowski, Józef, Dr. *Ignacy Jan Paderewski i odbudowa Polski* [Ignacy Jan Paderewski and the Rebuilding of Poland], Carl O. Jevert & Associates, 7517½ Coles Avenue, Chicago, Illinois, 1952

Paderewski, Ignacy Jan. *O Szopenie. Mowa wygłoszona na obchodzie szopenowskim w Filharmonii, dnia 23 października 1910.* [About Chopin. A Speech Delivered on the Chopin's Anniversary at the Philharmonic Hall on 23 October 1910]. Lwów, Wende i Spółka, 1911

Paderewski, Ignacy Jan & Lawton, Mary. *Memoirs*. Charles Scribner's Sons, New York, 1939

Parakilas, James. *Ballads Without Words. Chopin and the Tradition of the Instrumental Ballade*. Amadeus Press, Portland, Oregon, 1992

Parakilas, James. *Piano Roles: Three Hundred Years of Life with the Piano*. Yale University Press, 1999

Perkowska-Waszek, Małgorzata. *Ignacy Jan Paderewski. Letters to his Father and to Helena Górska (A Selection)*. Translated from the Polish by Cara Thornton. Presented and published in a symposium: "Musical Letters as a Reflection of Interregional Cultural Relations with Central and Eastern Europe."

Perkowska-Waszek, Małgorzata. *Ignacy Jan Paderewski o sobie—Zarys biografii wzbogacony listami artysty* [Ignacy Jan Paderewski About Himself—A Biographical Sketch Enriched by Artist's Correspondence].

Centrum Paderewskiego Tarnów – Kąśna Dolna, 2004

Perkowska-Waszek, Małgorzata. *Za kulisami wielkiej kariery: Paderewski w dziennikach i listach Sylwina i Anieli Strakaczów, 1936-1937.* [In the Shadows of a Great Career: Paderewski in the Diaries of Sylwin and Aniela Strakacz, 1936-1937]. Musica Iagellonica, Kraków, 1994

Phillips, Charles. *Paderewski—The Story of a Modern Immortal*. The Macmillan Company, New York, 1934

Phillips, James H. *Paderewski Discovers America*. Morris Publishing, 2006

Poniatowska, Irena. *Chopin and His Work*. Published in the Composers and the Art of Their Time. Adam Mickiewicz Institute, Warsaw, 2005

Pulit, Franciszek. *Dom w ojczyźnie* [A Home in the Fatherland]. Centrum Paderewskiego Tarnów – Kąśna Dolna, 2001

Ratcliffe, Ronald. V. *Steinway*. Chronicle Books, San Francisco, 2002

Rubinstein, Anton. *Autobiography of Anton Rubinstein*. Translated from the Russian by Aline Delano. Little, Brown and Company, Boston, 1890

Rubinstein, Arthur. *My Young Years*. Alfred Knopf, New York 1973

Rudziński, Witold, Ed. *Stanisław Moniuszko—Listy zebrane* [Stanisław Moniuszko—Collected Letters]. PWM 1969

Schoenberg, Harold C. *The Great Pianists From Mozart to the Present*. Simon & Schuster, 1987

Schoenberg, Harold C. *The Lives of the Great Composers*. W.W. Norton & Company, Inc. New York, 1970

Schumann, Robert. *On Music and Musicians*. University of California Press, Berkeley and Los Angeles, 1983

Schumann, Robert. *Schumann on Music—A Selection from the Writings*. Dover Publications, New York, 1988

Siwkowska, Janina. *Tam, gdzie Chopin chodził na pół czarnej...* [Where Chopin had his espresso...]. Książka i Wiedza, 1969

Słuszkiewicz, Edmund, Ed. *Wiersze o Chopine* [Poems about Chopin]. Polskie Wydawnictwo Muzyczne, 1968

Spóz, Andrzej. *Fryderyk Chopin: Mazurka in A-flat Major, Op. 7 no. 4*. Source Commentary. The Fryderyk Chopin Institute, Warsaw & the Bernardinum Publishing House, 2005

Steinway, Theodore E. *People and Pianos—A Century of Service to Music*. Steinway & Sons, New York, 1961

Strakacz, Aniela. *Paderewski as I Knew Him*. Rutgers University Press, 1949

Szulc, Tad. *Chopin in Paris*. Da Capo Press, 2000

Urbańczyk, Andrzej. *Pomnik Grunwaldzki w Krakowie* [The Grunwald Monument in Cracow]. Wydawnictwo Literackie, Kraków, 1974

Walczak, Bogdan, et al. *Geniusz przypadkowo grający na fortepianie* [A Genius Who Also Plays the Piano]; Wydawnictwo Naukowe UAM, Poznań, 2001

Wierzynski, Casimir. *The Life anf Death of Chopin*. Translated by Norbert Guterman with a Foreword by Artur Rubinstein. Simon and Schuster, New York, 1949

Weber, Bożena. *Paderewski*. PWM Edition & Parol Limited, Kraków, 1992

Zamoyski, Adam. *Paderewski*. Atheneum, New York, 1982

~ INDEX ~

Contains names of individuals, institutions, titles of musical compositions, historical events and geographical places found throughout the text

Górski, Wacław ("Wacio"), 117
Górski, Władysław, 27, 29, 64, 116, 117
Gottschalk, Louis Moreau, 4, 5-6, 139
Gounod, Charles, 42, 112
Granados, Enrique, 64
Grieg, Edvard Hagerup, 21, 52
     Piano Concerto in A minor, 21, 52
Grzymała, Count Wojciech, 106, 109, 110, 112, 126
Gyrowetz, Adalbert, 19

H
Hallé, Charles, 50
Handel, George Friedrich, 32, 63
Harasiewicz, Adam, 143
Haydn, Joseph, 6, 7, 59
     Symphonies, 13
     Variations in F minor, 63, 68
Heine, Heinrich, 125
Heller, Stephen, 122
Heschel, Georg, 88
Hesse-Bukowska, Barbara, 143
Heymann, Henry Sir, 56
Higginson, Colonel Henry Lee, 122
Hiller, Ferdinand, 39, 60, 61-62, 137, 139
Hitler, Adolf, 103, 121, 135
Hofmann, Józef, 143, 145
Horowitz, Vladimir, 6
Horszowski, Mieczysław, 6
Hôtel Lambert, 96, 97, 134
Hugo, Victor, 36, 126, 134
Hummel, Johann Nepomuk, 23, 33-34, 60, 80
     Concertos, 60
     Fantasy, 60
     Septet, 60
Huneker, James, 66, 88

I
Industrial Revolution, 7
Ingres, Jean Auguste Dominique, 36

Institute of Musical Arts (New York City), 145
Iwanowski (family), 17

J
Jełowicki, Aleksander, 109
Jeszcze Polska nie zginęła, 135-136
Joachim, Joseph, 27, 83, 96
Joseffy, Rafael, 66

K
Kalkbrenner, Friedrich, 37, 80
     Grand Polonaise, 37
Karlsbad (Town of), 50, 106
Kąśna Dolna, 95, 118
Kątski, Apolinary, 20, 21
Kenner, Kevin, 143
Kerntopf (Edward & family; pianos), 20-21, 85, 88
Kiev (City of), 17, 20
Kissin, Evgeny, 6
Knights of the Teutonic Order, 135
Koczalski, Raoul, 6, 138
Korsak, Antonina, 26, 107
Kraków (City of), 27, 28, 64, 101, 127, 135, 139, 143
Krasiński Palace, 19
Krasiński, Zygmunt, 96, 142
Kraszewski, Józef Ignacy, 89
Krzyżanowska, Justyna, 16, 18, 133
Kurpiński, Karol, 33
Kuryłówka (Village of), 15, 17

L
Lafayette, Marquis de (General Lafayette), 134
Lake Geneva, see Switzerland
Lamartine, Alphonse de, 36, 126
Lamoureux, Charles, 41, 97
Lamoureux Orchestra, 29, 116
Landowska, Wanda, 143, 145
Lanner, Joseph, 78

Marek Żebrowski began studying piano at the age of five. After graduating with the highest honors from the Poznań Music Lyceum, he studied with Robert Casadesus and Nadia Boulanger in France and Russell Sherman at the New England Conservatory of Music in Boston, where he received his Bachelor's and Master's Degrees. Hailed as "firm and eminently musical" by the Boston Globe, "strong and noble" by the Washington Post, and accorded highest accolades by the world press, Marek Żebrowski has appeared as soloist in recital and with symphony orchestras throughout the world. He has recorded works by Bach, Beethoven, Chopin, Debussy, Scriabin and Prokofiev for the Polish Radio and works by Ravel and Prokofiev for Apollo Records in Germany, and his performances and compositions are featured on the Titanic Records and Harmonia Mundi labels. Recognized as a composer with a catalogue of orchestral and chamber works, piano compositions and transcriptions, and film and stage scores, Mr. Żebrowski has received commissions from Meet the Composer and The New England String Quartet, among others, as well as composition prizes in the Netherlands. Mr. Żebrowski's works were premiered throughout the United States, Germany, Italy, The Netherlands, Poland, and South Africa. For the past several years he has collaborated with director David Lynch and their album of free improvisations, Polish Night Music, was released in April of 2008.

Marek Żebrowski has lectured for the Pacific Symphony Orchestra, Boston Symphony Orchestra, Harvard University, and The New England Conservatory of Music, and for several years was a contributing writer for the Boston Book Review. He has given master classes and has coached various chamber music ensembles and chamber orchestras. His academic career included teaching at the University of Massachusetts, the Massachusetts Institute of Technology, and UCLA. Currently, Mr. Żebrowski resides in Los Angeles and serves as the Program Director for the Polish Music Center at USC and the Artistic Director of the Paderewski Festival in Paso Robles, California. Marek Żebrowski is a Steinway Artist. He also authored *Paderewski in California* and several books about film directors and cinematographers, published by the Tumult Foundation.

~ Compositions by Fryderyk Chopin ~

Performed on Welte-Mignon Rolls
by Ignacy Jan Paderewski

1. Ballade in A-flat major, Op. 47 .... [7:56]
2. Etude in E major, Op. 10 no. 3 .... [4:40]
3. Etude in G-flat major, Op. 25 no. 9 .... [1:15]
4. Mazurka in B-flat minor, Op. 24 no. 4 .... [5:00]
5. Nocturne in G major, Op. 37 no. 2 .... [7:15]
6. Waltz in C-sharp minor, Op. 64 no. 2 .... [3:31]
7. Polonaise in A-flat major, Op. 53 .... [5:51]

Total time: [35:30]

[1] – [5]: Recordings from the Collections of the National Library in Warsaw, Poland
[6] – [7]: Recordings from the Collection of the Museum für Kunstautomaten, Seewen, Switzerland
Recorded on 27 February 1906

Played back and recorded in the Steinway-Welte, New York, Hamburg, 1925 (LM 71639)
grand piano in the Museum für Musikautomaten, CH 4206 Seewen, Switzerland, April 2001

Figure 43: The first partition of the Poland reduced the Commonwealth's huge territories; after two subsequent partitions in the 1790s, the country was erased from the map of Europe. Private collection. Used by permission.